"Exciting, dramatic, powerful, convicting. I read it in one sitting—couldn't put it down. The greatest blessing is looking over the shoulder of a matchless story-teller and seeing the power of an ancient Book break loose among a primitive people. It will restore your confidence in the power and glory of God's Word."

Dr. Joseph C. Aldrich,
President, Multnomah School of the Bible

"The deep truths all men are searching for are found in the Scriptures. Nowhere is that more clear—or more exciting—than in this gripping book. I've read a lot in this field. This is the best."

Bernie May,
Former Director, Wycliffe, USA

Dear Bethany,
this story blessed me so much and I had to order a copy for you! "Amazing how ALIVE & powerful Gods words are! Love, Dana

IN SEARCH OF THE SOURCE

A First Encounter with God's Word

Neil Anderson
with Hyatt Moore

MULTNOMAH

Portland, Oregon 97266

Unless otherwise indicated, all Scripture references are from the Holy Bible: New International Version, copyright 1973, 1978, 1984 by the International Bible Society. Used by permission of Zondervan Bible Publishers.

Edited by Larry R. Libby
Cover design by Bruce DeRoos
Cover illustration by Jerry Werner

IN SEARCH OF THE SOURCE
© 1992 by Wycliffe Bible Translators
Published by Multnomah Press
10209 SE Division Street
Portland, Oregon 97266

Multnomah Press is a ministry of
Multnomah School of the Bible
8435 NE Glisan Street
Portland, Oregon 97220

Printed in the United States of America.

Library of Congress Cataloging-in-Publication Data

Anderson, Neil, 1944 -
     In search of the source: A first encounter with God word/Neil Anderson and Hyatt Moore.
     p. cm.
Includes bibliographical references.
ISBN 0-88070-497-7 (pa)
ISBN 0-88070-534-5 (hd)
1. Anderson, Neil, 1944 - . 2. Missionaries — Papua New Guinea — Biography. 3. Folopa Language — Translating. 4. Missionaries — United States — Biography. 5. Bible — Translating. 6. Folopa (Papua New Guinea people) — Missions. 7. Wycliffe Bible Translators — Biography. 8. Summer Institute of Linguistics — Biography.
I. Moore, Hyatt. II. Title
BV3680 .N52A3 1992
266' .009953—dc20   92-6140
                                            CIP

92 93 94 95 96 97 98 99 00 01 - 10 9 8 7 6 5 4 3 2 1

Contents

Acknowledgments

We are grateful
for the assistance and counsel
of Sue Donaldson, Jane Pappenhagen,
and Larry Libby.

Foreword

Since before the Tower of Babel it's been an established truth that the best way to talk to anyone is in his or her own language.

Babel made the point in a negative way. Pentecost—something of a Babel in reverse—made the point again. That was Bible translation from heaven and an indication of the significance of the particular message. Since then however, the process of translating that message from one language and culture to another has been long and laborious. But it's not without deep value, high interest, and again, dependence on help from heaven.

Translating the Bible into a language that has never been written is no easy task. First the language must be learned—and that without the normal methods of textbooks and bilingual teachers. An alphabet must be devised, a grammar analyzed, and a complete word list compiled. To add to the challenge, it must be done on location, where the language is heard continually, and where there is a total immersion into the ways and means of the culture.

Not everyone has had, or would choose to have, opportunity to live among a far-off village people in Papua New Guinea. But that's what Wycliffe translators Neil and Carol Anderson have done, along with their four children, over a twenty-year period.

The Andersons realize that culture and language are tied together. It is not just words that a newcomer must learn, but what they really *stand for* in a given situation. Context has everything to do with meaning, and the context in which the Andersons came to work was very different from what any Westerner is used to. In fact, one of Carol's occupations while Neil was working on translation was to formulate and document a book of anthropological explanations of what makes the Folopa culture tick.

Did I say Bible translation was hard because of the language? It's also hard because it's the Bible. The Bible is an account of God's ways which, by God's definition, are not man's ways. This often makes for a clash. Something has to give, and God doesn't change. Such dynamics have been a reality throughout time, in all cultures, coming right down to our personal lives—penetrating, dividing joints and marrow. The experiences of such clashes portrayed in this book give insight into who we are as people, who the Folopa are as people, and ultimately into who God is as God.

Neil and I became friends during my brief (two-year) sojourn in Papua New Guinea. As we spent time together he shared with me some of his experiences and I determined they were worth sharing with a wider public. Though I lived in Ukarumpa, I went on a number of trips out to Folopa country and got something of a perspective of the Andersons' lives there. It's in that place, the end of the earth for most of us (but the very center for a certain few), that the book takes place.

Covering several years of time, the book makes a number of broad jumps to keep its focus. Needless to say, there was much more going on in the Andersons' lives during this period, like raising a family, taking further training, making trips back to the United States, keeping people who were supporting them informed, and handling the regular barrage of detail that fills every life anywhere.

While the Andersons' story is unique, it is also representational. There are many other couples and teams, as members of Wycliffe Bible Translators and the Summer Institute of Linguistics, as well as other groups involved in Bible translation, working in scores of other countries of the world besides Papua New Guinea. The accounts of each one are different, but each in its own way relates something of the explosion—indeed, the recreation—that takes place when God's Word merges with man's words in a language man understands.

It is to all of the teams still working toward that end that this book is dedicated.

Hyatt Moore

Beginning at the Beginning

(Genesis 1)

"In the beginning God created the heavens and the earth."

Bang! Stuck already!

Hapele, Isa, and I had just gotten started. We'd prayed, the pencils and papers were out, books were open, everything was ready—and now we were bogged down on the very first verse. But if you never start, you never finish. We even had a deadline approaching.

How do you say "created" in Folopa? That was a word I hadn't encountered yet. Usually I learned words by observing and by asking questions. If someone was cutting a tree I'd ask them what they were doing. They'd say *ni ditapó* and I'd write it down and work at lodging it in my memory. If they were cooking food or planting a garden, I'd stop and ask the words to describe it, always absorbing as much as I could.

But how do you come up with a word for something you've never seen? How do you even describe what you're looking for? I'd been up and down that village watching people, talking to them, picking up words, learning how they do things and why, but in all my time I hadn't seen anybody creating—especially not like that described in Genesis. Nobody was making something out of nothing.

Hapele, Isa, and I struggled, but without knowing what I was trying to get at, they could offer no word that was adequate. We had the word for "make" and "form" and "build," but none of these were quite it. We were not able to come up with the word that would express "bringing something new into being."

We decided to move on—maybe something would come later. Before we did, though, we prayed again. We asked God to somehow work out circumstances so we could discover the word we were looking for. There must be one in the Folopa language somewhere.

We continued with the translation but it didn't get much easier.

"And God said, 'Let there be light,' and there was light."

I had the word *dei* 'light,' but how do you say, "Let there be . . ."? Again, there weren't too many people doing things just that way or even using that expression. God's verbs are not man's verbs.

But He did it. He made the light, and He saw that it was good. And if He could do that, He could enlighten us. We translated it, but I wasn't so sure it was good. Not yet. But this was just a draft and we moved on.

We went on like that through the six days of creation until the seventh day when God rested. So did we.

There was a feast coming up and some of the men were preparing to go on a hunt. Hapele and Isa would be going, which meant that the translation work we'd just begun would be coming to a halt for at least a week.

"You wouldn't want to go," they said. "It's too hard. The hunting ground at Setu Wópu is very far away. It's very difficult to get there—very steep with lots of rocks, many leeches. You would never make it."

I knew by all this that they wanted me to go. So of course I did.

The next day we set out for the deep rain forest.

The trails in this part of the country are straight . . . straight up and straight down. And not exactly taxpayer-maintained tourist paths. Down in the rain forest where it never dries, half the walking is in mud, the other half is in streams. Trails lead through rivers and swamps, over fallen logs, across gorges, stair-stepping up or down cliffs, or climbing exposed tree roots hanging out of steep descents. The Folopa do it all barefoot, always at an unrelenting pace, racing against the ever-moving sun.

About midday we came to our first stop. Besides the shortness of usable daylight hours, the men don't like to pause much on a trek because of the ever-present leeches. When they stop at all, it's when they find a place that is relatively leech free, like a fallen tree suspended clear up off the ground. This day I had been ready for a break for a long time when we finally got to a tree like that. We all walked out on it and squatted down, lined up like birds on a wire.

I was really beat and there was no hiding it. One of the guys looked at me and said, "Héto Ali[1], you're going to die."

I took out my handkerchief, soaking wet just from being in my pocket, and wiped my forehead. I just looked at him. So I was going to die.

Somebody said, "Why don't you eat something?"

Those were welcome words. I'd been waiting for them to take the lead on this for quite a while. I was ready for lunch but nobody else was moving; everyone seemed to be waiting for me. Maybe this was only snack time. So, I'd take a snack. I knew I needed some nourishment.

I reached into my backpack and felt around. Everybody, including me, was curious about what special treat Carol might have put in there. I wasn't disappointed when I pulled out a big Cadbury chocolate bar wrapped in bright red, white, and brown. Bold across the front was printed the word "ENERGY." *Boy,* I thought, *that's what I need!*

In a culture where everything is shared there are no private pleasures for moments like this. I opened the end of the wrapper, bit off a chunk, and felt the gaze of forty eyes.

After a moment's quiet, me savoring, looking off into the rain forest, feigning oblivion to the eyes, one of the men spoke: *"Felére?"* he said. "Taste good?"

"Felérapó," I said. "It tastes good." And then, of course, "Do you want some?"

I hardly had to ask. And he hardly had to answer. He broadened his mouth and sucked breath through his teeth, the signal for "Yes, that would be really wonderful." I broke off a square and gave it to him.

Now forty eyes were on him as he relished the chocolate and ran his tongue around the inside of his mouth. A lick later somebody asked him, *"Felére?"*

"Brothers," he said in the Folopa language, "I'm dying of the deliciousness of whatever this is."

"What's it like?" they asked.

I wondered how he would answer. I could see the wheels turning in his head, his tongue still savoring over his teeth. To what would he compare this most different of tastes?

Finally he looked up. "It's like . . . pig's liver," he said.

Everybody hummed with satisfaction. I don't think I would have chosen just that comparison, but to them, it was the equivalent of the highest of the high. Of all the foods they get, pig is the best, and of the pig, the liver is the best part.

After that there was nothing to do but divide the bar into eighteen more pieces and pass them out. They took their bites, chewed, and sucked air through their teeth. Everybody agreed, chocolate deserved the pig's-liver prize for excellence.

That was the appetizer. After that I pulled out a sandwich and they reached into their shoulder bags and started bringing out all sorts of garden vegetables like taro and yam, precooked for the trip. Less sweet, perhaps, and without fancy packaging or "ENERGY" printed on the outside, but certainly containing more of the umph that would get legs and bodies up and down the hills in the afternoon hours to follow.

About dusk we reached an overhanging cliff—the kind of place they like to sleep under when out on the trail. Then if it rains—and it's likely to—at least they'll sleep dry.

I was sapped. Cadbury chocolate had long since left me, as well as everything else. We'd been going for twelve hours straight with just that one rest. My clothes had been soaked and resoaked with sweat. Mud coated my shoes, socks, and legs. Bright red runs of still uncoagulated blood from leeches added a bizarre aspect to my calves.

As we settled, the rain started. Before it came down hard, some of the men had gone off to gather firewood and whatever they could forage for supper. Some had found eggs buried in piles of decaying leaves, incubated by the heat. These finds are usually ninety percent embryo but still good for part of a meal. Returning, they made fires, cooked, ate, and prepared for the night.

It was cozy, all of us crowded together, the firelight glistening off the cliff at our backs, the rain falling like a sheet an arm's length in front of us, loud in the trees. When we bedded down it got even cozier. Twenty of us lay there side by side like sardines with me in the position of honor— right in the middle.

I was the only one with a legitimate blanket over me and a thin foam mat between me and the bumps underneath. Everybody else had odd assortments of sleeping gear: an old towel, part of a sheet, some bark cloth. Under them they'd put a few leaves they'd picked up on the way in.

Pretty soon everybody was snoring. The fires went out and it got cooler. In the middle of the night I turned over and realized that my blanket had been stretched into further service. Not only was it also covering the man on my right, but in part the man next to him, too. I looked the other way and it was the same thing there. There were five of us under that blanket.

I didn't do too much tossing and turning that night, nor did I do too much sleeping. But so it is sometimes the first night in a new bed.

It rained all night. Out before us was a vast ocean of jungle wetness. The small piece of ground under this cliff was the only dry spot in the jungle for miles around.

As dawn approached the rain lessened. A fog had rolled in. In the half-light, shapes were beginning to stir. Bodies were waking. As I lay there listening to the peaceful sound of drops falling on a thousand leaves, I heard a murmuring from somewhere down the row. It was somebody talking, half out loud, half to himself. As I listened I heard another down on the other side. Then another and another. The men were praying.

Though these petitions were meant for God, I didn't think anybody would mind if I listened in. I could just get the words of the man closest to me. It was Sopea.

"Lord," he was saying, "You know we're on a hunting trip and You know what we're after. All the game in the forest is Yours. If You want to keep it, that's up to You, but if You want to give some of it to us, that would be good. Help our hunting dogs. Don't let anything happen to them. You know how we need them. Don't let them die.

"And please take care of the women and children back in the village. Keep them safe. Don't let sickness come to our families. Protect them from enemies. Don't let the pigs get into our gardens and destroy them."

He went on like that for awhile and then I heard him pray about something else. "Concerning Héto Ali," he said, "You know we're all down here on the ground in the dark. You teach Héto Ali our language so he can give us Your Word and we can be in the light. . . ."

He kept praying but that was all I could get. When I heard it I was moved. There seemed a tremendous irony in it all. Here I was, the big white missionary, the one who had come all the way around the world to live among these people, to learn their language and their ways, and translate the Book. And here I was sandwiched between twenty hunters who knew almost nothing of God's Word, lying here on the bare earth but for a thin mat or a few leaves, and here they were spending their very first waking moments in prayer.

And some of those prayers they were praying were for me.

I was humbled. It would not be the last time.

2

Grubbing It Out

The following afternoon we arrived at Setu Wópu. That's a concise expression that means "the place now deserted where the Setu people once lived." The village of Setę had been leveled in a raid years earlier when the Folopa were still doing these things to each other. Now there wasn't much to show that a village had ever been there; the jungle reclaims everything. In such places, certain of the original plants will still be around, however, and remnants of gardens. That's why they make good hunting grounds. The old gardens attract the animals. Wild pigs will forage around for taro and sweet potato still growing. Setu Wópu was the best hunting ground for miles around.

Whatever they called it, I was ready for a stop. My feet were ready to get out of my shoes. But sitting back and resting for a while wasn't on the schedule. There was work to be done.

Everybody bustled with activity. First we had to build a shelter. The older men shouted commands to the younger, "Go cut poles, get thatch, get leaves, get rocks, get water, get firewood, get bamboo."

Some of the men immediately went off hunting—the first day always being the best before the animals became wary of our presence. A few cut down a sago palm and started chipping out the soft core, running water through the pulp, squeezing it out and catching the starch. That would provide the staple for our meals.

About dark it started to rain again. But the shelter was up and everybody moved in. The first afternoon of the hunt had been good, bringing in a couple of wild pigs and a big cassowary bird, a python, a tree kangaroo, and some other small game. The place was wild with chatter. Nobody gets excited like the Folopa, and the noise can be enough to rattle the faint of heart.

Amidst the clamor everybody went about the tasks of making fires, heating rocks for cooking, and preparing supper.

For me there was almost too much to take in: the skinning and gutting of the game, the scraping of bones, the smashing of skulls for immediate consumption of the brains (as these parts do not keep), the hanging of meat in the smoke over the fire to preserve and bring back to the village. Of smells there was a butcher shop's variety what with fresh intestines, burning hair, smoke, and cooking giblets, not to mention the locker-room aroma of our own bodies after the trek.

We were close together. The shelter was without walls,

about thirty feet long, the roof just high enough to get under. A pair of logs ran down its length and between them the fires burned. Men sat on either side sharing the heat for cooking and for warmth. I sat on some leaves, keeping dry, not saying much, just an occasional question to my neighbor—trying to take it all in.

Across the fire from me was Hotere, a short wiry man with a broad smile and about as tough as they come. With raw strength and a thirty-cent trade-store knife, he was struggling to disconnect the jaw from the head of a boar, cutting tough sinews, slicing the meat from the bones. Next to him another hunter, Kima, was singeing hair off what had been a tree kangaroo. Kayame braided some pig intestines to stick into a bamboo tube and cook. During a hunt they generally eat only the entrails, smoking and saving the rest for the feast back at the village.

At my left, Sopea was working on his supper. Out of his string bag he pulled a ball-shaped bundle wrapped with leaves tied together with tiny vines. I'd noticed others with similar leaf packages—filled with what, I did not know. This one seemed to be alive with movement inside.

When he got it open, I saw it was filled with beetles, about one hundred of them, bigger than walnuts, crawling all over each other, hissing, tangling their great pincers and spiny legs. Sopea took one, picked off its legs, and placed it just so in the coals, rolling it from side to side with a stick. Then he did the same with several more. In a few moments they swelled up and popped. Then he took one out, tossing it from hand to hand for a moment like a hot potato, and then popped it into his mouth and chewed it down.

Aware of my gaze in all this, he turned to me, his face about three inches from mine, and smiled—his mouth full of beetles and parts showing through his teeth. At that moment I decided it was time to change my focus and see what was happening on the other side of me.

Apusi Ali had a packet, too—another mystery-wrapped leaf bag tied in vine. He opened it up and spread it out. There, writhing and squirming, was a great pile of brown-headed, two-inch-long, white sago grubs.

Why, Lord, I thought, *of all places in this shelter, would I have to be sitting right here . . . between one man eating beetles and the other preparing to dine on grubs?*

Apusi Ali started scooping the grubs by the handful and funneling them into a bamboo tube, banging it down to pack them in. He plugged the open end with a piece of specially folded banana leaf and laid the tube across the logs to cook.

Again I knew it was time to turn my attention elsewhere. Anywhere.

Though I set my gaze at the farthest end of the shelter, with the corner of my eye I was still aware of Apusi Ali turning his bamboo tube of steaming grubs from side to side. Doing my best to avoid betraying any interest in this at all, I was still aware of his reaching back and tearing off a piece of banana leaf. I looked the other way. Still, I knew it when he laid the leaf out, took the bamboo tube off the fire, opened the top, and plopped the contents out in a big pile. Then, in spite of my fine performance of treating this activity like it wasn't happening at all, Apusi Ali, with the delight of a child at a birthday party, gingerly lifted the leaf by the corners and placed it squarely down in my lap.

Looking at me with a big smile he said, "Eat them, they're good!"

Suddenly the whole shelter became silent. You could have heard a beetle crunch, but even Sopea stopped chewing. The man down the log with the tree kangaroo rolled the carcass off the fire and stared. Hotere held his boar's head in his lap and they all watched me.

I looked down at the pile in my lap and up again. In the half-light of the place all I could see were eyes and gleaming brown faces catching the fire's glow. Finally, as calmly as I could, I said, "I don't know this food. How do you eat it?"

"Let me show you," Apusi Ali said. He picked up one of the thick, hot larvae and held it up to his mouth. Feigning to take a few tentative nibbles, he said, "You don't do it like this! That is the wrong way to eat sago grubs." Then, scooping up a great handful, he said, "This is the way to eat them," and he thrust the whole batch into his mouth.

He chewed, then he swallowed. As he swallowed, I did too, though my mouth was dry.

Then it was my turn. "Do you eat it with sago?" I asked, stalling as best I could. Sago is no favorite of mine either. Cooked, it's a rubbery, gelatinous mass—like something between tapioca pudding and a sponge. But here I just might need a sponge.

They thought the sago was a good idea. They love it. I thought of dishes I had recoiled from in childhood. What I wouldn't give now for one of those to trade for any of this.

Equipped with a bite of sago, I took a handful of the grubs, almost like Apusi Ali had done, inserted them in my mouth and chomped down.

As I chewed, everybody watched. I chewed for a long time, mouth closed, expression steady and finally they began to slip down my throat.

As I finished, Hǫtere leaned across the fire and asked, "*Felére?* Are they good?"

I paused, then matched his grin with my own and said, "*Felérapó.* Yes, they're good."

With that everybody burst into great cheers. People were slapping me on the back, waving and affirming emphatically, "Of course they're good. We just wanted you to know they're good!"

With that came a barrage of offers to taste every delicacy they had. Kayame gave me a piece of braided intestines skewered on a stick. Hǫtere gave me a bite of boar brains. So pleased they were that I would enjoy their food. But they were especially pleased that I would enjoy *o fóe* 'grubs.' And of course I had to eat some more.

At one point, genuinely interested, I asked, "What are these things, anyway?"

For a moment they looked at me incredulously. Could I be serious? What person in the world would not know what these were? I asked again and Kima leaned forward and said, "*Akaǫní o foe kaaratapo.*"

I only got about half of what he said. I'd heard *o fóe* in there and *akǫo*, the word for a large beetle, but the verb he used confused me. *Kaatapo* was the verb "to begin," I knew that, but I had never heard it with the *ra* in the middle. From other contexts I knew the *ra* infix, added to the verb "to begin," must mean "cause to begin," but I wasn't sure I had it.

"Wait a minute," I said. "What did you say?" It had gone by me so fast it was already blurred.

Soké, sitting next to Kima, piped up. Both Kima and Soké are astute with language, and they were always coaching me. Paraphrasing Kima's message for me, Soké pointed to the grubs on my right then over to the beetles on my left and said, "When these things fly, they fly as these."

I understood that fine. What they were telling me was that the sago grub is the larval stage of this particular beetle.

"But that's not what Kima said," I protested. I needed to hear the exact phrase again.

By that time nobody could remember it. It hadn't been that important. But, groping back, someone finally got it and this time I heard the whole thing good and slow: *Akaǥmí o fóe kaaratapó* 'these beetles cause these grubs to begin.'

I must have looked like I was catching onto something significant as they were all with me now. "Tell me more about this word, *kaaratapó*," I said, and everybody jumped in at once with all sorts of examples.

"You know," they said, "butterflies begin caterpillars. Flies begin maggots, rhinoceros beetles begin tree grubs."

When it quieted down a bit, Kima said, "It's like when the world started."

"What do you mean?" I asked.

"You know," he said, ". . . a long time ago. All this didn't just come up by itself. It had to have a beginning and somebody began it."

I looked at Hapele and Isa sitting a little way down from where all this was going on, and they too were listening closely. "We've been looking for a word," I said to everybody in general. "On the first day of translation we got stuck. We were trying to find a word that would describe something like what you're saying here but we couldn't find it—I think we're close, though."

"If we took the word for God, *Kóto*," I went on, "and added *ne* to indicate God as the one doing the action, then added *ra* in the middle of the verb, changing it from 'to begin' to 'to cause to begin,' what you'd have is: *Keké nále alimó Kótóné sąró haetamo Kaaralipakalepó,* 'in the beginning God caused the ground and the sky to come into being.' "

They nodded in unison.

"Just like that?" I asked. I could hardly believe it was falling into place.

"Just like that," they said.

Just like that God created the heavens and the earth. And just like that He had just given us a way to say it.

That night as I lay there again in the close company of the men whom I'd come to serve, I reflected on how all this had come together. Here we were, out on a hunt, miles from anywhere, certainly miles from the Bible house. Here I was in the unlikeliest of places to be doing linguistic work, crammed in at dinner between two men, one eating beetles and the other eating beetle grubs, and across the fire from two of the most linguistically gifted men in the village. And the words I'd been searching for from our first attempts at translation were plopped, like the dinner itself, right into my lap.

We had prayed about it that first day. We had needed a specific word and we had expected the answer to come somehow. I never quite expected it to be like this. But when I thought about it later, I thought, *how else?*

Genesis 1:1 was down. We had the beginning.

3

Before the Beginning

I wonder if I can really do this?"

That was the question I had the first day when I sat down and seriously addressed the project I was about to begin. I was in the Bible house. That's what the men called the little office we'd built across the path from the main house. It was still early morning and I was the only one there. The view of rugged, tree-laden mountains is majestic when clear, but now the only view was a wall of gray fog and with it came the chill.

How long had this been coming? All through college I'd dreamed of working in a place like this. It seemed ideal. I liked outdoor activities and this was outdoor living at its root. I liked mountain climbing, and now we were in the midst of mountains. I liked building things out of

wood and here I'd built not only our house but even all
the furniture that was in it. I've always liked people, and
there was certainly no shortage here—all very gregarious
and social. To add to all that, I've had a growing love for
studying the Bible, for getting to the bottom of what it's
really saying and relating its message to the events of
everyday life.

But now that I was here . . . *could I do it?* Could I really
accomplish what I'd been planning and dreaming and
praying and talking about for so long?

After attending BIOLA College, I went to Eastern
Washington University. I'd always thought I should be a
missionary. At least I could never think of any reason why I
shouldn't. I was a Christian. I was able. There was work to
be done for the Lord out in the world and I figured if anybody ever asked me why I didn't join in such a cause I
would not have any good answer. During my time at the
university that idea became more refined and focused into
a vision of becoming a Bible translator. I met Carol during
those days. She was going to Seattle Pacific University and
was following a similar leading to mine. So we joined ourselves together in marriage.

We took the course at the Summer Institute of Linguistics.
It was pretty grueling, but we made it through and applied
for membership with Wycliffe Bible Translators. As part of
that we were exposed to cross-cultural living and jungle
survival training in Mexico as well as all the rest of our orientation and preparation.

Once accepted by Wycliffe, we began speaking in churches,
telling our plans. We were going to serve the Lord—somewhere at the end of the earth. We'd see where.

Then we found out. Through "coincidences" here and

there, Papua New Guinea kept rising up and staring us in the face. "Five hundred languages," they said, "and most of them still unwritten." And those were all separate languages, not dialects! Since then the number has climbed to over eight hundred as more extensive language surveys have been taken.

We started investigating, asking people who'd been there. We talked to other translators. Some said it was a beautiful place with beautiful people. Some said the life could be hard. Both proved to be true.

It took us about a year and a half to get ready to go, getting our financing together and getting our gear. Heather, our oldest child, was five when we left and Dan almost two. The other two, Bruce and Wendy, were yet to be born in Papua New Guinea.

Getting settled in this tropical country wasn't without trauma. First we set up house at Ukarumpa. It's centrally located in the highlands and provides a place for language workers to stay when they're not in the villages. It's a comfortable enough place. Support staff live there year-round.

We were just getting into learning Melanesian Pidgin, the lingua franca used by a broad cross-section of people who otherwise don't share a common language, when Carol got sick. Actually, *sick* is hardly the word; she almost died. That's when I really wondered if we'd make it.

Carol had been weakening for some time but we didn't know what it was. Then one morning a friend came to visit. Alarmed by Carol's appearance, she contacted the only medical expert around at that time, David Lithgow. He had been a doctor but wasn't functioning as one then, having gone into Bible translation. He examined Carol and told us we needed to get to a hospital—fast.

She had some small boils under her arms and they weren't healing—nor was there any pus. This day though, the whole area was turning black as coal.

We left our kids with some good friends in Ukarumpa and tried to get a plane. They were all out. She couldn't go in a helicopter as she needed to lie flat. Finally we took a Datsun station wagon in which she could lie diagonally and we drove the two hours of dirt road to Goroka. All the way I was feeding her chips of ice for the sores that were forming in her mouth—and swelling at a rapid rate.

Carol held on until we got to the hospital. Then, as soon as the doctor came into the room, she lapsed into a coma. At that point nobody knew whether she was going to live or die. I was beside myself.

Her white corpuscle count had slipped to six hundred. It's supposed to be five to ten thousand. It was apparent to the medical staff that she was suffering from septicemia. Her bone marrow was simply no longer producing white corpuscles. Without those, any small infection cannot be countered and it takes over. That's why the boils had flourished and gangrene had set in, killing off that part of the body.

In the end we learned that she had been allergic to Camoquin, a malaria preventative that was in use at that time. It's since been generally replaced because of its risk to some people like Carol.

In the meantime I had nothing to do but pray. People back at Ukarumpa were praying. We had wired the States and people there were praying. Later we found that people all over the world were praying as one would contact another.

The coma continued day after day.

Every day I would come to the hospital, longing for news. But there was no news. There is no medical way to cause bone marrow to begin producing white corpuscles again once it has stopped.

Every day they would take a blood count and it would be the same. There was nothing to do but wait by her bedside, talking to her, playing music, praying. As days went by she turned completely yellow.

Then one day there was change. The lab technician who had been watching the count came running down the hall with the news, "It's up to eight hundred!" He was as excited as I was. Then the next day it was up more. Finally, at the end of a week she began to come out of the coma, slowly and incoherently, like out of a deep dream.

When she came clear, she wondered what the terrible stench was. I had to tell her. It was her own dead flesh. The gangrene was still there.

After that she stayed in the hospital three months. The gangrene had to be surgically removed and the area packed with bandages. Eventually they took skin grafts from the tops of her legs to patch up the big holes that were left.

There were multiple visits to follow, lasting a number of weeks at a time for the reconstructive surgery under her arms. Even after that she couldn't raise her arms over her head and had to have physiotherapy for months to get back her full movement.

The recuperation took over a year.

We were grateful for the medical team of Papua New

Guinean doctors and nurses who worked on Carol and put her back together, not to mention the scores of pints of blood donated by Papua New Guineans. (It's interesting to note that since then Carol has been unusually resistant to the kinds of diseases expatriates pick up in Papua New Guinea. We've wondered if some immunization came with all that native blood she received.)

What had mystified all the doctors who knew about the case was how Carol's bone marrow started producing white corpuscles again. For that we can only give God the credit and say it had to be a direct result of our prayers and the prayers of God's people holding us up.

In the end the head doctor told us, "It must have been a miracle."

We'll accept that. We do know it was a hard test for us. An early obstacle to get beyond to get doing what we came here to do.

When Carol got well enough to start caring for the family again, I began studying survey maps of the area where I thought we might go. Alex Vincent, a veteran field linguist from Australia, accompanied me as we walked all over a particular area of rugged highlands I'd seen once from the air. We were ten days on that trip, along with a Folopa interpreter I'd happened to meet in the city while caring for Carol. We'd sought permission from the government as well as the national church that was working in the area, and both were happy about our plans to possibly settle around there. So were the local people of the various villages. Alex and I talked with them, accepted their hospitality, and found out as much as we could about the situation. The place we chose was Fukutao, a hamlet of 350 Folopa people.

Not only did it seem right to us but there was a strong desire on the part of those people to have us settle among them.

I remember how the final meeting among the elders of Fukutao was both climactic and not. At such meetings everyone who has anything to say gets his turn with the older and wiser ones generally waiting to speak after those younger. Though I didn't know the language then and certainly couldn't follow the fine points of the dialogue, I could see that the considered opinion was highly favorable for our coming.

The most prestigious one among the elders, Owarape Ali—a fight chief and staunch representative of the old ways—spoke at the very last. He still had questions. He could not fathom that anyone would want to come out here and live with them. There was nothing to attract. I explained again how we wanted to live among them to learn their language and their ways and eventually translate the Bible so they could know the Lord and His Word for themselves. All this was still incredulous to him and in the end he just snorted and walked away, not really committing himself at all. I never knew what to make of it, but later others told me that it was God who had brought us.

The Folopa are a group of 2,500. They are native Melanesians, living in a particularly rugged area of the interior highlands. Their contact with anyone from the outside was comparatively late. Until about 1960 no "white skin" dared enter their territory, having heard tales of murder and cannibalism. By the time we came along in 1972 the Australian government had established a system of law and order, and there was already a church there.

The church had been established by an evangelist named Kirapareke. He was actually a Folopa by birth, but his village was destroyed when he was a child. He escaped with his family to a village in another language group, Samberigi. This village had a missionary and he heard the gospel and became a Christian. Later he became an evangelist and eventually went back into the Folopa area. He was the one who first introduced the Folopa to Christ. He lived with them for a while and taught them.

Before he left, Kirapareke told them to pray for a missionary to someday come to them. He assured them that God would hear their prayer. They prayed, and that, they said, was what had brought us—and that was why Owarape Ali had been powerless to speak against it. Without sharing the same language, however, it was difficult for the Folopa to get a grip on the message of the gospel. It looked like it was within reach—but it was actually just out of reach. There was a great deal of confusion.

On a second trip with Alex Vincent we started building a house, and a great many Folopa men pitched in with zeal.

We brought in a few things from the outside, but mainly we built it out of native materials: tree poles for the studs and beams, bark and split palm for the siding, sago palm leaves for the roof. By the time Carol and the children came, the structure was up and most of the floor was in, but there was still no water. The windows weren't finished either, which gave the villagers a good chance to find out who Carol was and observe our "strange" lifestyle. Our family all shared the same house, had no firepit on the floor, slept in beds, and the children slept apart from their mother. These were just a few of the things they found most curious about us.

As we settled, we got to know the people and worked at learning what we could of their language. The Folopa language is no easy one, full of sounds and mouth contortions native English speakers never make. It is full of nasalizations and glottal fricatives that come out sounding like a catch in the back of the throat. It is something of a tone language where two words spelled exactly the same will have altogether different meanings depending on whether they're said with a high pitch or a low pitch. Of course there were no books on the language and it was by our investigations we learned that it had fourteen vowels and fourteen consonants. We had to devise an alphabet.

Besides having different sounds, the grammar is different than we're used to in English. Verbs, for example, come at the end of a sentence or a clause. Sentence subjects are often merely implied and the listener must figure out by the context who is doing what. It's common, for example, for someone to say, "Went to work, felled large trees, lopped branches, cleared brush, made fence, returned to village," and you had just better know who's being talked about because no more hints will be given.

We gained friends and with that the necessary trust, without which we would be able to do nothing. Like everyone else we needed water and it was a long haul with buckets or gourds from the spring. They had never liked that either, so together we devised a plan for a pipeline. I was able to get a mile of plastic pipe and bring it up from the coast. They dug the ditch and before long we had a gravity-flow operation from a spring. Everybody was involved and everybody benefited.

We also did quite a bit of medical work. Not that we always knew what we were doing, but there was so much suffering we had to do something. Through radio contact with the doctor at Ukarumpa, rifling through health books, and having had an introduction to such in our field training, we learned as we went. We gave injections for pneumonia, treated seriously infected cuts and sores, tropical ulcers, malaria, and intestinal parasites. Later a volunteer dentist taught me to pull teeth, and I've since done a lot of that over the years.

Carol and I were involved in all this together. Besides her normal responsibilities of wife and mother, she had the added responsibility of teaching our children while we were in the village, using a correspondence course from the elementary school in Ukarumpa. And she also helped out with language data gathering, kept up the dictionary file, did all the typing, learned the language, and helped me a great deal with pronunciation nuances I wasn't hearing. Besides that she did more than half of the medical work.

We never knew what was going to happen next or what to do when it did, but we trusted the Lord, our wits, and experts back at Ukarumpa whom we could contact by radio. Not long after we first arrived, Carol was asked by a desperate mother to treat a three-year-old child who had rolled into the fire pit in the night. The fire had been out, but under the cooling ash, embers were still hot and a large area of the child's side and back was burned. The area had become infected and was covered with pus and flies by the time the parents brought the child to Carol for help.

It was a gruesome situation, but Carol gave herself to the child. After three weeks of intensive care, continually treating the infection, the child began to recover. Through these experiences our relationships with the people continued to deepen.

Of course our children were very popular among the

people and helped break down adult inhibitions and barriers. Heather went native. She insisted on dressing like a Folopa and wanted only a string bag and a doll for toys. From the time she first learned to read and write, she liked to gather a group of girls and sometimes even grown women together and hand out paper, pencils, crayons and books. She proceeded to "teach" them. Though her efforts were childish and many times she did not even know enough herself to teach them proper writing, many did go on to read and write. Dan, on the other hand, was very shy and wouldn't even venture to the front of the house for many weeks after we moved there. He played with some small cars on the floor and each day moved a little closer to the front door until he would finally play with a couple of children. Little by little he broadened his play area and circle of friends. Eventually he spent hours and even overnights in the bush on bird-hunting trips with his friends.

We had been there off and on for about two years when we received a radio message from Ukarumpa that a workshop was going to be held. We were to attend, along with a Folopa speaker, and bring ten chapters of first-draft trial translation ready to be checked. This was an SIL requirement of all new translation teams in the country. It would be taught by seasoned translators and consultants.

I'd known this day was coming, but still it took me by surprise. I didn't feel at all ready.

That's when everything went foggy for me and the chill came on.

Up until then, everything had been *go!* There had been the years of school, the training, the telling everybody back home of our commitment to do all this. There was the moving across the world, the settling, the almost killing sickness, the humiliation of starting again in first grade for learning everything in a new culture.

But now the real test was here. Didn't they know that for all our apparent good beginnings, I could hardly put two clauses together? This was too early. I wasn't ready. And I just wasn't sure I could really ever do it at all.

Out there in the Bible house that morning I prayed: "Lord, I just don't know how to do this. That one who spoke so confidently before, that must have been somebody else—some other Neil Anderson. This one is weak.

"Lord," I said, "I need help. I can't do this by myself. Will You help me? Will You tell me that You're going to help me? Is there some place in Your Word where You say You will? Show me where it is, Lord. I need a word from You."

The gray mist was still hanging low over the house and over my head, but out there above it I knew the sun was burning bright and warm. In time it would penetrate and the fog would lift. I opened my Bible and began to read.

After that I started every morning in the same way. Praying. Searching the Word for a word.

I read through several books of the New Testament until one morning I came to a verse at the end of Hebrews. It lifted me straight out of my chair. It was Hebrews 13:20-21.

May the God of peace, who through the blood of the eternal covenant brought back from the dead our Lord Jesus, that great Shepherd of the sheep, equip you with everything good for doing his will, and may he work in us what is pleasing to him, through Jesus Christ, to whom be glory for ever and ever. Amen.

Amen was right! I had found the word I'd been needing—equip. The Lord was promising to equip me. The whole passage qualified. Bible translation was a good thing. I knew that. And I had no doubt that our doing it was His will. He had gotten us this far and now here was the promise that He would equip me for what I would need to do next.

Gripping those verses like the oars of a life boat, I found Hapele and Isa, who had been coming to the Bible house and teaching me the language each day, and told them the time had come to start translating. Such an announcement was a highly significant thing for me, but they just said fine. I was almost surprised at how there was no apprehension on their part. But then, it's nice when you know a language from birth.

On the first day when we got into it, we started the session with prayer. In that prayer I claimed those same verses, Hebrews 13:20-21, as my rock of faith. I reminded the Lord of His promise: That He would equip us with everything good for doing His will. After that, every day when we'd start to work, we always included that verse in our prayers.

With that, and with full confidence on one side of the table and more than slight trepidation on the other, we forged ahead into our first work.

Genesis. The book of beginnings. Somehow, it seemed appropriate.

Beté: *The Source*

The Folopa are people of the earth. They live at ground level, close to the dirt, out of the soil. The creeping things are their meat. It's straight from the forest to the fire—no middle man. The ground sends up food to fill their bellies; when it goes lean, they do, too.

The Folopa aren't concerned with "getting back to the basics." They never left.

It should be no surprise then that the preeminence of things basic, of root issues, would be ever present in the Folopa mind. It's natural, like the body's need for water. It comes out in daily conversation, almost incidentally like a quick sip out of a bamboo tube. Sometimes it's part of a noun. Sometimes it's hidden between the tense and aspect in some verb. Sometimes it comes out in full strength and is addressed head on, occupying a full afternoon's discussion. Sometimes getting to the bottom of some issue can capture the energy and imagination of the whole village, and may dominate every conversation for days.

The term in Folopa is *beté.*

It's a word they use and use and use; it never gets tired, never old, never used up. Like words in any language, it has many moods, nuances, senses, shades of meaning. At once it embodies the concepts of root, basis, prime beginnings, deep structure, first cause, life, meaning, underlying strength, essence, source.

It is the fundamental verb of "being" and the most basic metaphor in the entire language.

Its uses are legion.

There are thousands of trees in Folopa country, tens and hundreds of thousands. With four hundred inches of rain per year, they grow huge and fast and thick. They provide heads for their arrows, bark for their clothes, boards for their houses, fuel for their fires, poles for their fences. They also provide unwanted shade. In Folopa country open space and sunshine are in demand.

When Folopas begin to clear undergrowth for a new garden—as they do at least yearly—the biggest part of the work is cutting down and clearing away the trees. With arms like steel bands and their one-and-a-half-pound axes, they besiege a trunk until the towering height finally gives way with a crash. For a while the plot intended for the new garden looks worse than ever, the tree now claiming not just the sunlight but the ground itself. But the men aren't done. The tree subdued, the axmen dismember it, and clear it all away.

But there's something they know about all this process: cutting down a tree does not kill it. Like weeds they keep coming back. Everything from above the ground may be dead and rotting but the part that's left below is still alive. A season later new shoots will be up, sprouting at one side or the other out of the trunk. A force below the ground has determined again to reach for the sky.

That, they know, is where the life is. The top part, the part that shows, the part that one can point at and call tree, that's not where the life is. The life is at the base, in the bole, under the ground where you can't see.

The Folopa know that if you haven't dealt with that, you haven't dealt with the real issue.

There's good reason for the Folopa's consuming interest in things beyond the visible. Very little of the food they eat comes from above ground. Three of their four staples, sweet potato, taro, and yam, all come from below the surface. And the fourth, sago, comes from deep inside the trunk of a palm.

Folopa terrain is craggy, rough, and honeycombed with caves. Rivers and streams follow contours and crevasses, taking any route as long as it's down, often dropping into a hole in the ground to run underneath, sometimes for miles, before appearing again. When the Folopa follow a stream to such a place where it just appears out of the ground, that place is called the *beté* of the stream.

The word for teeth is *sereke.* At least that's the name for visible teeth, the ones in front. But the big ones, the ones in the back of the mouth, are called *beté sereke.* The teeth in the front are seen, but the *beté sereke* are hidden, and they're the ones that do the real grinding.

Sometimes the *beté* must be removed. One time we had a problem with wasps. There were hundreds of them—big, red-bellied menaces about an inch long—nested deep in the bole of an old tree stump just off the main trail. These wasps are lethal. When they sting it's like an ice pick going in. When children get stung in the face they swell up so badly they can hardly be recognized. When an adult gets stung the pain will last for three weeks.

To get rid of them we tried insect poison, but the wasps were not fazed. We poured gasoline down the hole they'd made to the surface and lit it. There was a whoof but again, the wasps were untroubled. The nest was in the ceiling of the bole where the roots connect and nothing could reach it.

As cursory measures were not working, the men took it on like a mortal challenge. Pumping each other up with courage like they would do for battle, they covered themselves with cloth and leaves and, brandishing branches to ward off attack, they moved in with fire. That weakened the stump. Then, continuing to dance back and forth in and out of harm's way, they dug the ground all around, cutting through the roots. Finally they were able to split the stump open and expose the nest. As the wasps swarmed Sopea reached in, grabbed the nest, and jerked it out. As he held it aloft there was a cheer of victory. Later they ate the wasp larvae and chrysalides that came with the nest.

But, though well damaged, the tree trunk with the hole was still there. More wasps would come back. They continued their work of excavating the stump, finally pulling it out of the ground and rolling it down the long slope into oblivion. After that there was no more problem. They'd gotten the source. The *beté* was gone.

There's a system of justice in these villages. If someone's been wronged he can call the appointed elders, usually one from each of several villages, and they'll determine the case. During the trial they'll want to hear the story from each point of view, listening for indications of motive. The motive will usually explain the crime and determine the guilt. Without the motive made plain there's nothing to try. They've got to come to the *beté*.

Differences are often handled less formally than calling a court. When grudges surface in a close society they're handled in the open—out in front of everybody. The Folopa can be volatile and fights can arise for any number of reasons—the same lusts and wants that war in the members of the whole human race. When a person has a grievance against another, he or she will stand in the common area in front of the house of the accused and start shouting it out. When that happens ears perk up all over the village. Pretty soon the accused will appear and start shouting back.

As the crowd gathers, threats fly like arrows. One of the contestants may grab a club or an ax and it'll start to look bad. Before any real damage is done, however, everybody will have gotten into place.

Everyone knows their role in these situations. The clan brothers of the one will gather behind to restrain him from doing actual harm to the other. The clan brothers on the other side will do the same. With this kind of safety the two fighters can begin to go at it with murderous energy yet without anyone suffering mortal injury. As often as not one of the clan brothers will get the worst of it through jabs and bites to the point of even losing half an ear or a couple of teeth.

When these kinds of things happen, the commotion is incredible. As there's no getting anything done until it passes, I usually go watch with everyone else. I stand off to the side and without fail someone will see my interest and come up to me and ask, "Do you know what's going on here?"

Having arrived after the beginning I'm at something of a disadvantage, but I venture a guess.

"Let's see," I might say, "Kopo is saying that Apusi's pig got into his garden and ate a bunch of his taro plants. And Apusi is saying that even if it did that didn't warrant Kopo coming and cutting down his banana trees. And now Apusi's threatening to dig up the rest of Kopo's taro. But Kopo's saying if he does that it may be the end of Apusi's pig."

With a little glint in his eye my friend will look at me and say, "Yes . . ." and then, "but, no. What you're saying is right, but there's more to it. Do you want to know the *beté* of this fight?"

I'll say, "Sure," and what he'll tell me is something completely separate from what's on the surface—something that may have been seething for some time before a pig got out of hand. In this case maybe Kopo's sister had been promised to Apusi but at the last minute she had married someone else. Such an action would upset everything. Besides the personal blow, the balance of bride exchanges is upset, not to mention bride price[2] which affects the whole clan. The older brother might have been the one responsible for letting this happen, complicating the matter. Finally, a pig ran rampant in a garden and the whole thing blew up and all that yelling about pigs and taro plants is really about something else. The earlier reason is the *beté* of the fight.

Words have a *beté*, too. The Folopa are continually teaching me the language, and I'm continually learning it. Someone can be moving through a monologue, complete with the rapid-fire series of flaps and nasals and trills, and I'll be following along with understanding until a word or an idiom goes by that I've never heard before. Either the speaker recognizes that he's suddenly left me in the dust or I stop him and ask for a meaning.

"You want to know the *beté* of that word?" he says, and I'll say yes, and he tells me. The *beté* of a word is its meaning.

All things have a *beté* and until you know what it is, you're only dealing on the surface. Yet besides this, there is another side of meaning to the word. In listening I've discovered they use it in reference to people, at least certain people. These are individuals who have tapped into something that gives them strength. They seem to have self-sufficiency. Sometimes a man always seems to have enough money, shells, food, or pigs. When there's a feast he always has the most to share. He never runs short. "That man," they say, "has *beté*."

All this adds another dimension to the term. Whereas to know *beté* is being on the road to wisdom, to have *beté* can be a goal in life. It can become a quest. People want to know What is out there that will last? What is self-propagating, inexhaustible, ultimate? And how do we tie into it?

As in any society, among the Folopa there is a tyranny of false *betés*. Futureless hopes. Incorrect assumptions. Myths with confused morals. All these tend to undermine and counter honest attempts at grasping reality. If the basis is wrong, how can good grow from it?

In past times, and still today among some, personal *beté* came from the bones of a dead man who had been powerful.

The one who possessed those bones was thought to have the ability to control the spirit and gain access to its power.

Absorption with the concept of *beté* in the spiritual sense, then, has been pervasive in all Folopa history. They've always known there was another reality, a reality behind the physical dimension, and that reality had more power than anything they could wield in their natural state. They were afraid of it, had a deep regard for it, and were perennially curious about it.

It was to this mind and this world view that Kirapareke the evangelist had first come and introduced a new Power. Though invisible, this Power was stronger than anything they had ever feared—yet amazingly was interested in their good rather than their harm.

This was the *Beté* behind all the *betés* they had ever imagined and almost too good to be true. Those who believed found evidence within themselves that it was so.

It was this great *Beté* of *betés* we now had the privilege of exploring—together.

Afterward, none of us would be the same.

5

Women

(Genesis 2)

After God had created a few things out of nothing, He put some others together with elements already made.

Out of the ground He formed the beasts of the field and the birds of the air.

Out of the dust He created man.

And out of man He created woman.

Women have no easy row to hoe in the Folopa garden. They're very much the burden bearers of the society. All day long they work their plots, bending and pulling and digging. In the evenings they haul the produce home, bent under the weight of their string bags hung over their backs from their foreheads. The walk may be an hour long, over steep, slippery terrain. Under such loads they can't move their heads from side to side—they can only look up from under their eyebrows. But as burdened as they are, while they're at it they may also bring a bundle of fire wood on their head or carry a baby in yet another string bag across their front.

It's not unusual to see a small woman weighing under one hundred pounds carrying a one-hundred-pound load up a mountain trail. She's strong and she knows it. It may be all too much but this is what she's born to. She won't complain, at least not out loud.

Back at her hut she does the cooking for her family. When it's available, the Folopa eat great quantities of food. For the women, there isn't much protein around. Not being the hunters, they often get only the rats and the insects. Before Christianity was introduced, there were numerous taboos against women eating meat at all. Working bodies require enormous volumes of tubers and greens. With such intake comes increased intestinal size and enlarged abdomens. Sometimes it's difficult to tell if a woman is pregnant just by looking at her.

The women bear the burdens and the women bear the babies. The body she's given is not only for herself, but also for her husband, her children at her skirts, and her baby at her breasts.

Moreover, the women's roles are highly restricted in Folopa society and they are well aware of it. While their bodies may be strong, socially they are powerless, at least compared to men. Even in legends they are always the disadvantaged. If a couple does not have children it is always the woman's fault.

Traditionally, there has even been some doubt as to whether women were of the same species. They are born the same way, yes, but where did they come from originally? How did it come about that in so many ways women should be so different from men?

Though we were translating Genesis, it was "revelation" for the Folopa. We were working on chapter 2. God had been creating all things and systems to keep them all operating. Before He was through, He planted a garden complete with trees and rivers and everything good for the stomach as well as the eye, and He put the man He had made in the garden to work it. Then, seeing there was something missing even before the man did, He said, "It is not good for the man to be alone. I will make a helper suitable for him."

Just that quickly we were delving into the origin of women.

God caused a deep sleep to come over the first man. For the Folopa that's an appropriate beginning of anything. Dreams aren't just late-night movies. These people know that things happen in your sleep. Of course there's nothing said about dreams in Genesis 2, and the Folopa have never seen a movie, but when Adam woke up things had changed. He was no longer alone. Where there had been one of him there were now two—and he may have had a pain in his side. We translated:

Then the LORD God made a woman from the rib he had taken out of the man, and he brought her to the man. The man said, "This is now bone of my bones and flesh of my flesh; she shall be called 'woman,' for she was taken out of man" (Genesis 2:22-23).

We worked through all that, one concept at a time. Then I read it back to see if it made sense. It did—and much more than I could have realized.

Hapele and Isa leaned back from the table and looked at me.

"Wow," Isa said. "So women were made from men."

I nodded.

"Bone of my bones, flesh of my flesh. She came out of man. She got up out of his sleep. She was pulled out of his side and she's been at his side ever since."

"Then," Hapele leaned forward and said, "the *beté* of woman is man."

I nodded, not yet sensing the profoundness of the revelation this would be for the Folopa people.

As the word got around the village of what the Scripture said on this matter, another new beginning took place in Folopa. Women began to take on a new esteem. Seeds of new dignity had just been sown. Just as the Judeo-Christian ethic, when truly applied, has always elevated the role and the condition of women, it was happening again right here in Folopa country.

Genesis 2 laid it out: Women are not another race. They are of man, bone and flesh, created by God, coequal in value.

The *beté* of woman is man.

And beneath that, the *beté* of woman is God.

6

The Beté of Hard Work

(Genesis 3)

Hapele, Isa, and I looked out the Bible house window. It's not really a window—more like part of the wall that opens like a big flap with a rope and a pulley. When it's open it adds space to the small office and gives a spectacular view of the valley falling away beneath us. With jungle-covered mountains to the horizon, the terrain is rough, but majestic—like Eden after the caretakers were gone.

We'd been with Adam and Eve all morning. God was there too, handing down the curse. Pre-lunch hunger pangs were jabbing my empty stomach, which was grinding, trying to digest itself. We were ready for a break but discipline kept us going just a little longer.

Adam had fallen. He'd bitten the fruit. The serpent had fallen and he'd bitten the dust. Our first forefather, representing us all, had broken the law and God was obligated to punish. As a race we wanted our eyes opened—to have knowledge of good and evil—and this was our price to pay. We hadn't known how good we had it until we knew evil, and then it was too late. Now we knew evil, and the consequences of disobeying God were set in motion for all time.

As for Eve's part, God decreed pain in childbearing and told her: "Your desire will be for your husband, and he will rule over you" (Genesis 3:16).

No surprises for the men there. We continued on.

To Adam he said, "Because you listened to your wife and ate from the tree about which I commanded you, 'You must not eat of it,' Cursed is the ground because of you; through painful toil you will eat of it all the days of your life" (Genesis 3:17).

As we worked through that, I noted that Hapele and Isa's attentions had gone out the window. Quiet as the distance, their minds were on something. My stomach growled again. The humidity was climbing and it was getting hot. I glanced at my watch and moved on.

It will produce thorns and thistles for you, and you will eat the plants of the field (Genesis 3:18).

Thorns and thistles are familiar realities. In this country sting nettles are a bane of the trail. The path gets rough in places and if you put your hand out to steady yourself, or brush a bare leg against a bush, you may have a painful reminder for hours. Bare Folopa feet are vulnerable to thorns, no matter how calloused and tough the soles.

We trudged on. Just one more verse of the curse, then lunch.

By the sweat of your brow you will eat your food until you return to the ground, since from it you were taken; for dust you are and to dust you will return (Genesis 3:19).

There. We were finished for the morning.

I moved my chair to get up, but Isa was gazing out the window again and Hapele was looking down at what we'd just worked through. He read it out loud, "By the sweat of your brow you will eat your bread. . . ."

"Yeah," I said, "what does that mean to you?"

Hapele looked up at me, paused for a moment, and simply said, "Nothing!"

"I don't get it either," Isa pitched in.

"You don't get what?"

"This part about the sweat of your brow. What's that have to do with anything? What does it mean, 'You eat food with it'?"

I looked again. The words were right, the grammar seemed pretty good. Maybe it was the idiom. "You don't eat food by the sweat of your brow," I explained, "but that's how you get your food."

"Oh."

"Do you understand it?" I asked.

"No."

We were both perplexed. It seemed pretty straight-forward

to me. How could I explain it any clearer? Then it hit me. These people don't associate sweat with work. I noticed the small beads of sweat on Hapele's forehead. It was the same on Isa's. Here in the tropics where temperatures can soar and the humidity with it, you don't have to work to sweat. You can perspire just sitting in your houses. We were perspiring now.

I tried again. "The ground is cursed," I said, "and because of that, man now has to go through great strain to get anything out of it; it's going to tax all his strength."

I knew it was part of the Folopa world view that they are under some kind of a curse—that there is a punishment out there for something, which they're suffering under. All this is a central theme to their thinking, but its origin has always been a mystery to them. They have a few myths about it but nothing very satisfying.

Hapele turned his faraway look back to me. "That's really true," he said. He pointed broadly with his chin. "Do you see those gardens out there?"

Yes, I saw them; not that they particularly stood out. They were tiny in the distance and appeared about as rough as the rest of the terrain but for the cleared trees.

"*That's* hard work," he said. "But we have to keep at it. Food doesn't come up by itself. There's not much food coming up by itself in the jungle. Maybe some berries. But sweet potatoes, taro, yams—they don't grow by themselves. That takes hard work. We've got to make gardens. We've got to cut down huge trees, chop off the limbs, and clear it all out of the way. The trunks have to be rolled off to the edge and stacked up for fences to keep the pigs out." He looked back at me. "That's really hard work."

"Right," I nodded. "And you work up a sweat doing it."

"I suppose," he said, "but we don't say that."

"What do you say?"

"We say, *depe tukó walapó* 'We burst our stomach.' "

Now there was an expression I could relate to. In colloquial English, we'd say "busting your gut." And it fits—out there in the gardens you can hear it, the men cutting, hauling, digging, heaving. Muscles stretch like bands, teeth clench, vessels bulge, throats grunt, stomachs break.

We crossed out what we had on the draft and rewrote it.

No longer will your food just come up by itself, but by bursting your stomach you will do your work, raise your food; and you will go on like that until you die and become part of the ground again (Genesis 3:19).

With that, it all made sense.

We took our break for lunch and by the sweat of my brow I was ready for it. As we separated, Hapele and Isa lingered a bit with people milling about around the path. In fact, they called a small crowd together. I overheard some of their conversation.

"Do you know what?" Hapele and Isa were saying. "It is God that has us under this curse. That's what we translated today. It was because of the first people. They disobeyed. They ate what they weren't supposed to eat, even though it came up free.

"God punished them so nothing would come up free anymore. That's why it is that only by bursting our stomachs we get our food."

That's all I heard of it, but I could see that another new

understanding had come to the village that day and one more significant than I might have realized. I grew up knowing these things so I couldn't always foresee when there was going to be a significant breakthrough in understanding. For them this was a new *beté*—and an understanding of the basis for the human predicament.

I sat at lunch and talked to Carol about it. I was tired but content. We had both put in a full morning, me at the translation table with the men, Carol in the house with the children and their schoolwork.

But, like God—when He'd finished His work, looked at it, and called it good—I was satisfied.

Only we weren't finished. Not by a long shot.

7

Custom Curses

(Genesis 3 and 4)

In many ways the Folopa understanding of the world is clearer than the understanding of the Western mind. Perhaps it comes with a certain freedom from all the distractions that we hold so dear. Perhaps it's because these people live so close to the earth that they're continually aware of how dependent they are on it. In truth we all are, but we tend to forget. The Folopa never forget.

When God said to Adam, "Cursed is the ground because of you," the Folopa shudder with its truth. When God told Cain that because of his sin against his brother when he tilled the ground it would no longer yield its crops for him, the Folopa react with silence. That's how they respond when they're most deeply moved.

They understand these things all too well. It's part of

their world view that when a person or a community sins, the ground will go bad.

That ground is not just "earth" as we usually think of it. It's not a matter of soil analysis. It's on a more basic level and has to do with all that makes living what it is and all that makes a village a village. Everything ultimately comes out of the earth. To the Folopa it's like "mother." In fact in Folopa, the word for earth and the word for mother are the same.

When the earth goes bad, life begins to stop. In Folopa ritual, the most important practice is the festival to make the ground good. They will prepare for it for weeks. As they do, the men will sleep inside a special round house used only for this purpose, over special stones, sanctified with colored markings buried in the earth. During those weeks there will be no working, no chopping of wood, no loud noises. If all the practices are not done correctly, the ground will not be good. Many still believe this.

If people start dying, they know that the ground has gone bad. Whole communities have been known to move to another area when this has happened.

We were still in the early chapters of Genesis.

The LORD said, "What have you done? Listen! Your brother's blood cries out to me from the ground. Now you are under a curse and driven from the ground, which opened its mouth to receive your brother's blood from your hand. When you work the ground, it will no longer yield its crops for you. You will be a restless wanderer on the earth" (Genesis 4:10-12).

We worked through it and I put my pencil down. As another verse was translated, another picture of God was painted on Folopa canvas. Here we saw how God does not just effect curses in a broad, general way, as He did with Adam and Eve, the result of which extended to all mankind. He also custom shapes these things, tailoring them individually for specific sins.

Hapele and Isa had been following the story with great interest. The two brothers' theme is preeminent to Folopa folklore.

Cain and Abel had brought offerings to the Lord, each from his own area of labor. Abel brought fat portions from the firstborn of his flock. Cain brought fruits from the soil. The Lord had looked with favor on Abel and his offering but on Cain and his He didn't. Clouds gathered outside of Eden and Cain's countenance blackened.

In spite of Cain's sacrifice not being accepted, the Lord did show patience with him.

Then the LORD said to Cain, "Why are you angry? Why is your face downcast? If you do what is right, will you not be   accepted? But if you do not do what is right, sin is crouching at your door; it desires to have you, but you must master it" (Genesis 4:6-7).

There was Cain's challenge: to master the temptation to sin. He had a chance to back up and try again—to pick himself up and go on. He could still master the situation. But if he let this disapproval get to him and let bitterness begin, he would be the one mastered.

As we went over this, Hapele and Isa and I talked about the principles that were coming through, principles they also observed. How much, for example, of any bitterness against our brothers has its genesis in our own faults, not theirs? How many of our resentments toward others really stem from something God is trying to do in our lives?

Cain's argument had been with God, but he turned his back on Him and took it out on a person. All God wanted Cain to do was kill an animal. Instead he became one, killing his brother.

We translated on.

Then the LORD said to Cain, "Where is your brother Abel?" "I don't know," he replied. "Am I my brother's keeper?" (Genesis 4:9).

In Folopa culture, where family and clan ties are everything, Cain's answer was an affront. God took it that way, too.

God cursed Cain.

Though Cain was a farmer—and a good one—from then on when he worked the ground it would yield nothing for him. That was the pronouncement. Bringing produce from the ground wouldn't just be difficult like it is for everybody; for him it would be impossible.

The ground had swallowed the blood of Abel and now it was clotted over for Cain. His new destiny was to become a restless wanderer on the earth.

When we finished the passage Isa said, "It's good. Very good. But one thing troubles me. Blood . . . it doesn't have a voice. And the ground . . . it doesn't have a mouth."

He had a point. The trouble is, that's what the Bible says. It was a use of personification—giving animate attributes to inanimate things. Lots of cultures and languages use it and it can be powerful. But when a language doesn't—as the Folopa doesn't—having the ground open its mouth and blood speak words tended to make a fairy tale out of the whole teaching.

They looked to me for some answer that would make sense and all I could do was look to God. I admit that I felt something of a consternation with God. These were His words, yet it seemed they just wouldn't translate.

"Lord," I prayed, "we've got a problem. You're the one who said this. You're the one who used personification. It worked fine in its setting. You know what You meant, the Hebrews who first had it knew what You meant, I think I know what You meant, but how do we get these Folopa to know what You meant? If You could not have used personification in the original version, how would You have said it? Or, specifically, how shall we say it now?"

As we discussed the dilemma at the table, the answers started coming. Hapele and Isa had the basic understanding. Cain had slain his brother and it was no secret. He might have thought it was; he tried to pretend he didn't know where his brother was, but nothing is a secret from God who sees all. The blood of Abel that soaked into the ground was evidence of Cain's guilt. It was like a court case. God was the judge, the plaintiff was Abel (or the blood of Abel), crying out for justice and retribution. It was as if Abel was saying, "God, you are the judge of the whole earth; do something." An innocent had been violated. It wasn't right. The guilt demanded a just punishment. The demand for justice is a clear and basic concept in Papua New Guinea cultures. They call it "payback." God could not, and cannot, allow sin to go un-paid-back. Though Abel was now powerless, God was not.

As we drafted the translation we used that term, "payback." We wrote:

God said, "Cain, you killed your brother secretly, but I saw it. Now you must be paid back for what you have done. You killed your brother and his blood went into the ground. Now I am going to curse the ground for you because of what you have done."

Maybe in the future, in some subsequent version of the scripture translation, personification of the blood and the earth will communicate well. For this moment, however, such only confuses. Whichever way we choose to say it, the truth remains. God sees all and does not let wrong just pass.

That could be gloomy, but fortunately Genesis is the beginning, not the end. The story goes on. History has continued. Since then the blood of Another has been spilled on the ground. Blood that, as the book of Hebrews says, speaks a better word than the blood of Abel. From a Man on a cross, blood ran down and the earth opened up its mouth. Again, that blood speaks of vengeance, but this time also of mercy. The vengeance was covered; the payback paid for.

But we were still in Genesis. The best was yet to come.

8

The Magic of the Written Word

This was an epoch-making day. People were crowding all around our house, talking loudly. They were excited because actual bound books with printed words in the Folopa language had reached their village for the very first time. And they wanted to see them. This was the beginning—a whole new page of history.

From the time we first started living among the Folopa people we explained who we were and what we had come to do. We told them that we had come to learn their language, write it down, and then teach them how to read and write. We said we would be recording their legends, history, and stories about their daily lives. Ever since then they were always highly motivated and anxious to get involved with anything having to do with "school," or what they thought school must be—never having had any experience of what school actually was.

At the time we did not know all that was behind that motivation. They had apparently heard reports from the outside world about their fellow citizens going to school and then getting jobs and making unheard-of amounts of money. Whatever the reason, their enthusiasm was remarkable.

Over the months of language learning, they saw us writing things down in books. They were waiting for the time when they'd "have the knowledge of books." Each time we returned to the village from a stay in Ukarumpa, they'd say, "Did you bring the books?" We'd have to tell them we didn't have the books ready just yet.

But then, after we'd been at it a couple of years, before our first furlough, Carol and I attended a beginning literacy workshop at Ukarumpa. We took in lectures and worked with the language helpers we had brought with us from the village, Momako and his wife, Numiame. Together we put Folopa stories together. Our third child, Bruce, was born in the middle of the four-week course so Carol missed one week, but she made it back the last week to finish the first Folopa reading primer. Carol drew the pictures and did the layout for printing. Bruce did his part by sleeping most of the time.

The primer consisted of sixty-nine lessons, each with a simple drawing to illustrate the word containing the letter to be taught in that lesson. The book was very simple, about 120 pages long. The total cost of the primer, along with a notebook and pencil, was about two dollars.

Literacy experts recommend a maximum of twenty-five students for a trial literacy class. (These are called trial literacy classes because the alphabet needs to be tested and approved before greater volumes of literature are published.) So, having produced this primer at Ukarumpa, we brought it back to the village.

As soon as the two language helpers climbed out of the helicopter they started telling everybody, "We've got the books!" The word shot through the villages in a heartbeat. We were attempting to carry our children and belongings the hundred yards or so from the helicopter pad to the house when we were suddenly mobbed.

"Where are the books? We want to see the books!"

They were in a very unimpressive little box, and I wondered if these people were still going to be so excited when they actually saw them. Then Momako and Numiame, who had been with us, came and said, "Come on, show them the books. They want to see the books!"

We were so tired from the long, hot day of traveling to the village. We had planned to just move in, unpack, and get things cleaned up. Thatched-roof houses always have lots of debris falling out of the thatch from the wind, covering beds and everything else in the house. Cleaning up is quite a job. We weren't expecting to do anything except get settled in. But there were so many people crowding around with so much enthusiasm and loud talking about these books.

"When are you going to start school?" they demanded.

"Tomorrow," I shouted above the din. "And that's the good news. The bad news is that the maximum number of students allowed in this course is twenty-five. We will change it to twenty-six because there are thirteen clans. Choose two people from each clan and that's all who can come. The decision will be in the hands of the village leaders. What's more, it's not free—the exercise book, primer, and pencil you get is going to cost two dollars."

Their excitement wasn't abated a bit. They still wanted to see the books. So we opened the box, held up a sample of the contents, and then went into the house. They went off and had a long discussion.

After about three hours, all the headmen came back to the house and announced they had decided who would get to participate in the class. I got some paper on a clipboard and wrote down the thirteen clans, one at a time, listing the names of the people as they called them out to me.

When we finished I said, "Okay, now these chosen men must pay two dollars for their books and will have to be here tomorrow morning." Money isn't that easy to come by in this part of the country. They can sometimes get money by selling trapped cassowary birds to another language group who value the feathers as well as the meat. But then, there's not that much to spend money on either. So when I said they'd have to pay two dollars each they immediately produced the money. We gave each of them their books.

Carol and I went back inside the house, but the crowd was still milling about outside. They were ready to begin school right then. They were a very loud bunch, talking, looking at the books, carrying them around. Now and then they'd call out that they wanted to start school, RIGHT NOW! And I had to say, "*No!* We are not starting school now, we're waiting until tomorrow morning."

They weren't very happy about that news. But gradually, over the next hour and a half, they dispersed.

So we got the cleaning and unpacking done. We were

just beat—dead tired. We went to bed, collapsing under the mosquito net. The kids were sound asleep.

Before dawn the next morning, Carol pushed on me.

"Neil, wake up. There are people all around outside the house."

I crawled out from under the mosquito net, went to the window and looked out. I could hardly believe what I saw. People were strutting around with their books under their arms and their pencils in their hair.

They noticed that I'd gotten up. They were all out there trying to be quiet, making more noise trying to be quiet than they were before.

They were saying, "Shhh! The white man's asleep, don't make so much noise!"

So I came out and said, "What's going on?"

"That's okay," they said. "You go on sleeping, but when you're ready, we're out here!"

It wasn't even six o'clock yet! We got up, brushed our teeth, and dressed. As we went about our daily morning routine of cooking oatmeal, getting kids up, and contacting Ukarumpa on the radio schedule, the noise level outside just kept going up and up and up. More and more people kept coming, like this was *the* event of the day!

By the time breakfast was over and it was supposedly time to start, there were about one hundred people, all jammed around our porch. I could hardly get out through the door and across the path! I had my book and was thinking about how I was going to pull this off—not only getting out the door and squeezing my way to the Bible house but also teaching these men to read using my limited Folopa.

I reached the door and thought, what are all these people here for?

"I said only twenty-six!" I shouted above the clamor.

"That's okay," they said. "We know. The rest of us just want to watch."

I managed to get myself into the crowd, and suddenly there was a commotion. A man was elbowing his way through, dripping with sweat, his chest heaving. A young boy followed him. He got about three inches from my nose and shouted at me.

"What have you done? You've sold all the books to these clans, but you didn't count all the clans. I belong to a different clan. You left us out, and we're part of this village. I'm the last one left of our clan and this is my only son. You've got to let him in here!"

I looked at the other clan leaders. "Is this right?"

They said it was. He was one tiny remnant of a clan and he was making his point.

Everyone stared at me, wondering what I was going to do. I'd already made concessions to have twenty-six in the class. I looked over at Carol and asked her if we had any more books. She said there were a couple left.

I studied this young boy. He was small, twelve or thirteen years old. He was looking up at me with an intense, pleading, hopeful look, like all the future of his whole eternity hinged on me and my decision of this moment. He had washed himself, put on his best pair of shorts and held some kind of piece of paper to make himself look like a student. I told his father it would cost two dollars for the books and pencil. He reached in his pocket and handed over the money in a flash. So Carol got the book, note-book, and pencil for him and we continued working our way through the masses over to the Bible house.

All we had in those days was a blackboard and some crude benches we'd made out of bush materials. Here were twenty-seven would-be scholars, sitting, not knowing which way to hold the book, most not knowing what to do with the pencil. They weren't sharpened and they didn't know how to sharpen them. There were about a hundred people hanging in the windows and door, wanting to observe whatever wonder was about to follow.

We started off on lesson one. I did my best with my limited Folopa to teach the very basic first lesson. I pointed to the *i* in the word *diki* (bow) and said, "This says 'ee'." Then I pointed to the *i* in the other word, *dika* (yam) and said, "This is the part of *dika* that says 'ee'."

I was going through all this in the best Folopa I could muster. They followed my attempts with intensity, their eyes glued on my every move. Classroom learning was a new concept. To them, pedagogical methods were new. They seemed to be expecting some sort of magic. They were sitting, watching. Holding their collective breath. Waiting for the magic to hit. It was bound to happen within those hallowed four walls of school!

For me the work was utterly draining. It took so much strength to get through that first lesson. We went over it about ten times, trying ten different approaches and they were all saying *"Ee, diki, diki,"* louder and louder, thinking maybe if they said it loud enough they'd somehow get it.

Finally, after a couple of hours, and me completely exhausted, I said, "That's it. End of lesson one. End of school for today."

They all looked at me, dead serious, boring holes in me with their eyes. A self-appointed spokesman rose to his feet. "You're bad," he said heatedly.

"Why?"

"We've heard of other places where they have school and they have it all day long. We want to have school all day long, too."

"Fine," I said. "In other places they have school all day long. But here, today, this is it! Tomorrow we're going to have lesson two. If you want to learn some more, go outside and look at the book, look at the pictures, and read it over and over and over." I was tired and I wasn't going to do any more.

After that those men showed up every day, on time, for all sixty-nine lessons. Some of them never got it. Some of them always figured it was some kind of magic and that you had to hold the book in a certain way or look at it in a certain way, and that would do it. About four or five of them, however, did learn to read (including, by the way, the little guy from the smallest clan who had wanted so badly to be included).

The village was amazed. Some believed the magic was indeed powerful—that some actually had learned to read. We agreed it was a wondrous thing. It was their learning to read that really gave us our start. After that they could instruct us in the parts of their language where we had imperfect understanding. They corrected some of the spelling we had devised. Cooperative efforts in that area are what have made the Folopa spelling system really work.

———◄●►———

After that, people who had not been in class would come to those who knew how to read begging, "Come on, give me the secret of reading, give me the power." So they taught one another.

One man, though, virtually taught himself. His name was Awiame Ali.

From the beginning Awiame Ali took us under his wing and would tell us the inside scoop on cultural things we found confusing. He was one of our best friends. Though he was chosen to be one of the two from his clan to go to the first literacy class, and though he went through it all faithfully, he didn't learn a thing. And it discouraged him.

He was about thirty-five, but he'd had something like polio when he was younger, so his legs were as skinny as sticks and he walked stiffly with a stick. But he was very strong from the waist up. When we were building our house in the early days, he came and said, "Look, I'm a lame man. I can't go to the bush to get logs and bring them back on my shoulders. But I will do what I can for you. I will dig a hole for your outhouse." And he did—over fourteen feet deep!

He wanted so badly to know how to read. When we finished translating Genesis, we made five copies and left them with the men who knew how to read while we went on furlough. Awiame Ali's desire to read was so strong that he talked one of those out of his copy of Genesis. He would come alongside those who could read and say, "Here, read this to me." He would read the primer and Genesis together. He took his copy of Genesis to the garden, to the bush, and wherever he went—fishing or hunting. It was his constant companion and he would go over and over it.

One year later, when we came back, as we were moving back into the house and cleaning up, Carol said, "Neil, what's that sound?" She went over to the door and said,

"Awiame Ali is on the back porch, reading! It sounds like he's reading Genesis!"

"That's impossible," I said. "He can't read."

I went out there and sure enough, there he was, sitting on the porch reading the book of Genesis. We went outside and gathered around him.

"Awiame Ali," I said, "can you read?"

Beaming and proud, he told us the whole story.

The light that beamed in Awiame Ali that day on our porch has spread to others in the village as they continue to teach each other to read. Further light has shone among the villagers as they come to realize that determination and hard work, not magic, is the key to gaining the power of the written word.

9

Bad Raps in Egypt

(Genesis 37-45)

Joseph was a dreamer. He started dreaming in Genesis 37 and then lived those dreams out for the next dozen chapters.

The Folopa love the story of Joseph. In the days when we were translating it, there was lots of talk about Joseph in church and around the village. They strongly identified with him—favored by his father yet put down by his brothers, given dreams of future glory but shunned and falsely accused in the meantime. Yet, through it all, his character was faultless, and his trust was in God.

Hapele, Isa, and I had been to the translation workshop and when we returned we threw out the whole first draft and worked it over again. Ten more men had joined in the process, with others coming from time to time.

At our pace of working, often stopping to analyze words,

explain culture (both Folopa and biblical), and continually working out the grammar, it wasn't exactly a thrill a minute. But the slowness and the continual discussion enabled all of us to stand in awe of the content and deep meaning of every passage.

Joseph had hit the pits. His brothers had thrown him in, and there he might have stayed until his bones bleached, but for one brother's better idea that they sell him into slavery. Twenty pieces of silver wouldn't go far among ten brothers, but it would get him off their hands and would free their conscience of murder.

Joseph was alone in Egypt but God was with him. That was apparent in everything he did. Though he'd been humbled from his former position of favored son, he was faithful in what was put before him. He made an excellent slave. He was sharp, organized, a natural leader. He picked up the new language, handled mathematics, finances, and people. Besides that he was young, good-looking, and well-built. He had *beté.* . . .

Potiphar, the captain of Pharaoh's bodyguard, bought him in the slave market and put him to work. In time Joseph was in charge of the whole place: house, fields, slaves, finances, everything—except the food Potiphar ate, and his wife.

The only problem was the wife. With her husband often gone and no housework to do, she had time on her hands. What was there to do but lounge around the house all day in her Nefertiti frocks? And that hunk of Hebrew slave looked better to her every day.

The story got more interesting every day. For the Folopa, ratings for this soap opera could top any of the charts. We translated:

Now Joseph was well-built and handsome, and after a while his master's wife took notice of Joseph and said, "Come to bed with me!" (Genesis 39:6-7).

"How's that?" the men interrupted.

"She said, 'Come to bed with me.' You know . . . 'Lie with me.' "

They looked confused. In my plainest Folopa I reworded it. "She wanted to have sexual intercourse with him."

"Oh," they said. "But we don't say it that way."

"How do you say it?"

"We say ẹ saasepe." That translates, "get me."

Fair enough. I wrote it down that way and we moved on.

"Get me," she said. And though she spoke to him day after day, he refused to get her or even be with her. Next verse:

One day he went into the house to attend to his duties, and none of the household servants was inside. She caught him by his cloak and said, "Get me!" But he left his cloak in her hand and ran out of the house (Genesis 39:11-12).

Everybody at the table was struck by the moral strength of Joseph. Certainly he had passions like everybody else, he was young and alone and had suffered much. Here was his opportunity for pleasure. And with the privacy, who would know anything?

Ironically, in our discussions, we got hung up for a moment about the place of privacy. In Papua New Guinea cultures where houses are small and families are large, sexual relations are relegated to the garden. The cover of the bush is the only place that is private. When Potiphar's wife tried to get Joseph inside the house and he ran out to the garden to get away, it all seemed reversed.

But that's the way it was there. Some places are just different.

We translated the next section:

When she saw that he had left his cloak in her hand and had run out of the house, she called her household servants. "Look," she said to them, "this Hebrew has been brought to us to make sport of us! He came in here to get me, but I screamed. When he heard me scream for help, he left his cloak beside me and ran out of the house" (Genesis 39:13-15).

When we got to that last part, all the men in the Bible house, already on the edge of their seats, leaned forward and with one voice yelled, *"That's a lie!"*

Fists clenched, jaws tightened, veins bulged on necks. It was a scandal! How could such a man, so upright, so guileless, be treated this way by a "no good" woman? Then it got worse. In the next paragraph, when Potiphar came home, he believed her. Potiphar burned with anger at Joseph and the Folopa burned with anger at his wife and the injustice of it all. But no words are recorded of any defense from Joseph as he was hauled away to prison.

Day after day the men came—watching to see how Joseph would get out of prison and become second-in-command in all Egypt. In spite of what was on the surface, the man really did have *beté.* God had let things seem to fall apart, but in the end, He showed that He'd had control all along.

After we had finished Genesis in first draft, we got a new group of men together for a checking session. We were going through it all again with people who had had no previous exposure to the translation to make sure it was communicating clearly. We read it aloud. Carol was there in the Bible house, too, typing revised manuscripts, just managing to stay ahead of us as we read along.

Joseph made a real impact on this group, just like with those who worked on the first draft.

There he was, falsely accused, imprisoned, but always rising to the top in spite of bad situations. He was a dreamer, and dreams are significant in Folopa culture. He had been wronged by his brothers. Relationships between brothers figure very prominently in Folopa legends. The apparent intrigue and deception between them after Joseph got out of prison and became leader in Egypt was just their kind of meat.

Joseph wasn't telling them who he was. He demanded that they bring their youngest brother Benjamin if they were to ever see his face (and get food) again. Then when they did, he tricked them in a false accusation of stealing where Benjamin was implicated and heading for jail. The brothers knew they had hit bottom at that point and the Folopa very much identified. The brothers knew that they had finally met with justice for the sin committed against their brother so long before. (They still did not know that that very brother was standing before them.) The Folopa feel this same heaviness that the brothers felt. Among them the knowledge that they stand in a position of continually deserving punishment is a common theme. The brothers were guilty of spilling innocent blood and now it was coming back to haunt them. The Folopa feel that all the time.

Folopa culture corresponds with Old Testament culture in many ways, and this is one of them. There is a very strong bond between father and son—and a particularly unique one with the youngest son. The Folopa call him "the milk-stops baby," and they could identify with Jacob's great reticence to give Benjamin up. The news of Benjamin's imprisonment, once it reached the father, really would bring down his life in bitterness and sorrow.

Finally, Judah, who had promised his father he'd guard Benjamin with his life, begged Joseph to let him take Benjamin's place.

Still checking for clarity of translation, we read:

"So now, if the boy is not with us when I go back to your servant my father and if my father, whose life is closely bound up with the boy's life, sees that the boy isn't there, he will die. Your servants will bring the gray head of our father down to the grave in sorrow. Your servant guaranteed the boy's safety to my father. I said, 'If I do not bring him back to you, I will bear the blame before you, my father, all my life!' Now then, please let your servant remain here as my lord's slave in place of the boy, and let the boy return with his brothers. How can I go back to my father if the boy is not with me? No! Do not let me see the misery that would come upon my father" (Genesis 44:30-34).

I looked up to see if the text was communicating. The men were silent, sitting cross-legged on the floor in their ruggedness, some shirtless, expressions dark, chests heaving. I saw one brush a tear from his eye.

I read on. After that, Joseph could no longer control himself either. He, too, knew of the special bond between father and youngest son. He, too, knew that if the brothers returned to the father without the youngest son, the father really would die. But when he saw the loyalty and the love, that the older brother was willing to take the sentence of the younger—and was pleading to do it—Joseph broke down, went to the other room, and wept aloud. When he returned he confessed who he really was—their own brother.

At that point we had reached the end of the page. Carol was still typing the latest draft and we had caught up to her. For the moment there was no more to read and, as it was time for a break anyway, I went and busied myself with tea and bread for everybody.

But behind me all remained quiet—all but the typewriter. I looked back. There were the men gathered all around Carol, reading the words one at a time, as they came onto the page from the typewriter.

The tea and the bread could wait. They, apparently, had food I knew not of.

By the time the page was finished, Joseph had told how he had known his brothers all along, that he remembered their sin against him but that he was not going to work payback on it, but rather he had seen how God was using him to help them when they needed it most.

At this point one of the older men looked up at me. Putting his hand to his throat in serious Folopa gesture he said, "We are dying of the deliciousness of these words." He picked up the paper Carol had just finished and read a verse.

"And now, do not be distressed and do not be angry with yourselves for selling me here, because it was to save lives that God sent me ahead of you" (Genesis 45:5).

He looked around at the others and then out the window. He spoke slowly.

"The brother whom they had most greatly offended," he said, "was in the end the one who had the most power to destroy them. Yet he passed it over. Instead he became the one who rescued them." He sighed and said, "There's a great *beté* here."

10

Looking for Love

(John 3:16)

We were standing in about a foot of water, in a river, in the dark, deep in a cave, and the men thought this would be a good time to stop and pray.

It had been good weather, not too much rain, and a good time for hunting bats. The water level would be down in the cave where the biggest bats live. Though the Folopa like to eat the smaller ones, too, they really like these big fruit bats, the ones with a wing span of two and three feet.

They usually go into the cave through a large cavern at the opening. This time I suggested we go in the other way. I didn't flatter myself that they had invited me along on this expedition because of my hunting prowess. More likely they hoped I would bring my battery flashlight, easier and more efficient than their flaming torches.

The cave goes all the way through the mountain, though at the entrance I proposed, the opening is very narrow and tight with a river running in. You have to wade in about four feet of water with only a foot of air space to the ceiling. They had never been that way, which for me was all the more reason to give it a try.

We'd made it through the long entrance and found it opened up to a series of large rooms. Though it got broader and shallower, there was nothing to do but keep wading in the water. It was fairly easy going and I was a little surprised that they wanted to stop here and pray. Even those who were not prayers by habit or believers at all wanted to pray here.

Fine, I thought, men ought always pray and not faint. This was as good a place and time as any.

A couple of them led out. It was quite solemn, beseeching God for protection in this unknown place, particularly from anything that might live in it. From a couple of them I heard the word Sowé but didn't think anything of it. I'd never heard it before, but at that time there were still a lot of words I hadn't heard yet. It was later I learned more about the source of their gnawing apprehension. In earlier years this had been a burying river.

In those days, before burying underground became mandatory by law, they had a variety of ways to do it, depending on what they wanted to do with the spirit.

In Folopa belief, the spirit of a person is in the bones. After death it still lingers on with the bones, knows the kind of treatment its body is shown, and thereafter has power to manifest and work in ways beyond human means.

This is one reason people would always show great mourning besides the normal reasons of genuine bereavement, and why special treatment was given the body.

For a person who had lived honorably, an honorable burial was given. They'd place the body up on a platform a little distance from the village. The women would then climb the platform every day and with branches of leaves keep the flies off the putrefying body. Finally the women would eat it, a part at a time.

But for a person who'd died after being only a nuisance and pain to the village and whose spirit was not wanted anywhere around, they gave this one no burial at all. Instead, after a little superficial mourning, they would build a platform over a river—this very one, which goes into the mountain and disappears—and burn the platform, body and all.

When the platform crumbled, it was all swept away into the mountain—flesh, bones (spirit), and all.

That river was the one we were standing in now.

After praying we went on. In time we came upon the bats, hanging upside down from the ceilings, their little red eyes eerily glinting in the flashlight rays.

When bats are seen in a Folopa cave, everything else is forgotten. The place erupts with wild excitement, everyone yelling, shooting, and climbing about on the rocks, holding their balance with stalactites and stalagmites. With the wild echo chamber of black bats flapping madly and black men yelling at the top of their lungs deep in the black earth—it all becomes a madhouse.

"Shine the light over there!"

"No, shine the light over here!"

"I hit one, he's there in the water!"

"There's one carrying a wounded bat away! Get them!"

"Watch where you're shooting. *I'm* over here!"

Folopa bird arrows are multipronged; the bows are made of palm, strung with a strip of bamboo. The arrow itself doesn't usually kill, but impales the bat and brings it down. As it flops around in the water while trying to swim, the hunter picks it up by the shaft of the arrow. Folding the wings back, he removes the arrow and finishes the bat off by bashing its head against a rock.

The bats retreated deeper and deeper into the cave and we kept up the pursuit. The passage narrowed, the water getting deep in places. We kept moving, though I sensed some of that same apprehension I had noted before. Still, the excitement of the hunt kept everybody going.

When finally it widened out again we found ourselves in a huge cavern. We stood on the sandy shore of an underground lake surrounded by sheer walls.

"This is it," everybody said. "No more road."

It was true, there was no going around the lake, but we were already drenched in water so what was the problem? Why not go on? The flashlight beams showed the bats hanging from the ceiling on the other side. I wondered why they would give up now.

"Wait a minute," I said, "we don't know about this lake. It may not be very deep."

"No," they said, "don't go in there."

"Why not?"

"Just don't. We're at the end. No more road."

"But the bats—they're right over there. That's what we came for."

Nobody moved. I didn't understand it. We'd been in the river. What was the difference between a river and a lake? Finally I moved in.

"I'm just going out to see if it's deep," I said. "Maybe it's very shallow."

"Don't!"

The protest came from all ten. I didn't understand. These were tough men, rugged, ready for anything. We had traversed worse than this before.

I got about a quarter of the way out and called back, "It's only sand." The water was up to my waist and they were watching me with eyes wide and faces sober—like they were never going to see me again.

Folopa people feel very responsible for one another, never letting another go alone on the trail, and taking full responsibility if something happens to a traveling companion. I didn't think of it then, but my venturing out alone in this unknown place was laying great stress on them.

I continued out to the middle. The water came up to my armpits and then, as I continued to step ahead, it started to shallow out again. I kept moving and finally came to the shallows on the other side.

"Here I am," I called. "It's no problem. Come on."

Finally, Apusi Ali ventured in. Apusi Ali is only four foot eleven but about as tough as they come. If he were a football player and the coach told him to tackle a Greyhound bus, he'd do it. With his bag half full of bats held aloft in one hand and his bow and arrows in the other, he set out.

The skill of swimming is hardly known among the Folopa, even when they don't have their hands full. In a minute or so of careful wading he was up to his neck and he called out, "Am I half way?"

"Sure," I said, "come on."

The water was black as tar and was up to his chin with his head turned up before he finally hit the gradual up-slope and slowly trudged on out.

With him safe on the other side, all the rest came across together. One kicked something that moved which gave him a start and he yelped. Picking it up, he found it to be a human bone. Others found some, too. That didn't help to calm the nerves much, but once we were on the far side there was nothing to do but go on. That was our purpose in any case.

The excitement rose again as we went on hunting bats. We followed them farther into the cave, getting one here and there until we reached a sheer, vertical wall in front of us. Off to the side was a hole where the river raced in. There was no going any farther. By then we'd had enough, so we carefully retraced our steps, came out of the cave, and went home.

We were a long way from John 3:16, the verse we'd started working on the day before—but the hunting had been a good morning's diversion. Back at the house I got all the muck off, went in, took a shower, and had lunch. That afternoon Hapele met me in the Bible house to resume translation.

Carol and I had been living with the people some four

and a half years at that time and we were just about to take our first furlough. We'd translated Genesis in first draft and a few other Old Testament passages, but we hadn't translated anything from the New Testament. We still had a lot to learn, and I still didn't have the word for "love," or, for that matter, "perish." But I wanted to give it a try, if only just this verse, before we'd leave the area for a year.

For God so loved the world that he gave his one and only Son, that whoever believes in him shall not perish but have eternal life (John 3:16).

John 3:16. How many call this the central verse of the Bible? It's the bottom line of the whole message, in many senses the *beté*.

Before we settled down to work that afternoon, I still had some questions about what had been happening that morning.

"Hapele," I said, "there's something that puzzles me. I know you guys are pretty tough. This morning I saw you all scaling the walls in that cave, scrambling around in the dark without even a flashlight, grabbing those big screaming bats with your bare hands. But what I can't figure is why everybody was so slow about crossing that little lake."

Without a moment's hesitation he said, "Sowé."

"What is Sowé?"

"You mean, '*Who* is Sowé?' "

"Okay, who is Sowé?"

"Haven't you heard the legend of the two brothers?"

I had not—at least not this one. As a matter of fact, I hadn't even heard the word for "legend" and I'd been trying to get it for some time. I had been taught by our anthropologists that you can learn a great deal about a people from their legends. But up until then I had not been able to make much inquiry as I didn't even have the word. *Deté fele fo* is the term, "the talk that goes on and on." I wrote it down.

Hapele's face became dead serious as he began.

"There were two brothers who went fishing in a small lake. They made a raft like we do when we fish. The older one stood on it and scooped water onto the shore as fast as he could with a big sago frond. Every now and then he scooped up a fish. The younger brother would grab it before it could squirm back into the lake.

"After a while the older brother got tired and he said, 'Hey, younger brother, I'm tired. Let's switch places. You come here and scoop and I'll come over there and have a smoke.'

"So they changed places. The younger brother was scooping away when the older one looked up and said, 'Hey, you're sinking.'

"Sure enough, the raft was under water and the younger brother was up to his ankles. 'You'd better come out,' he told him.

"The younger brother took his sago frond and tried paddling the raft to shore. He paddled for all he was worth but it wouldn't move. By then the water was up to his knees.

" 'Brother,' the younger one called out, 'something's down there! It's got the raft and it's got a hold of my ankles. It's pulling me in!'

"With that the older brother flew into action, doing

everything he could think of. He threw vines to the younger brother and they pulled together, but the vines broke. He found a long pole and held it out. They pulled with all their might, but nothing budged.

"Both of them were yelling, entreating the other, panicking. The younger was in water up to his waist and still going down. Then he was up to his armpits, his shoulders, his neck. Finally, when only his head and forearms were above water, he suddenly ceased his flailing. While he still had his mouth above water he called out, 'Brother, *koneo!*' and disappeared.

"As soon as he was gone the older brother took off running as fast as he could. He went to the village and his clansmen, calling, 'Clansmen, Sowé! Sowé has gotten my brother!'

"The clansmen rose immediately to action. Quickly they grabbed the largest pig they had and, running it back to the lake, took their axs, split it open, and threw it into the water, yelling, 'Sowé, here's your pig!' "

Hapele stopped. Then he looked at me like what he was about to say was the most significant part of the whole story.

"Do you know what happened then?" he asked.

I had no idea.

"Nothing," he said.

"Nothing?"

"Nothing. Sowé sucked the man down and there was nothing he or his brother could do to keep him up. And when the clansmen came and offered him the pig, their best pig, the best sacrifice they had to appease him, he didn't take it."

"So the man died," I said.

"He did more than die. He was pulled down into the deep forever. He perished."

"What?"

"He perished."

I wrote it down. *Aluyalepo.* It was one of the very words I'd been needing. I was getting somewhere, right on time, but Hapele continued.

"People don't go near that lake now," he said. "They don't fish in it, they don't whisper near it, they don't even make footfalls anywhere around it." He looked at me hard. "A man-getting Sowé lives in that lake."

I was beginning to realize how serious this was.

"I thought you said that was a legend," I said.

"It is," he said. "But it really happened."

We both sat silent for a moment, then I asked, "Does everybody know that story?"

"Everybody knows it."

"Does everybody believe it?"

"It happened."

This is incredible, I thought. There's a thing in the lake, some creature down there that gets people. It's some weird force, evil, and beyond human control. The only thing that might appease such powers of the other world is some sacrifice. A pig is the best they've got and a valuable thing, but when they give it, nothing happens.

It was a lesson for life, a warning of great and hostile powers in the dark places of this world and that the means by which men can deal with them are only paltry and in the end, ineffective.

But this came with later reflection. For the moment I was still gathering words.

"What did he say before he drowned?" I asked.

"*Koneo.*"

"What does that mean?"

He shrugged his shoulders. "It's just *koneo.*"

Farewell, I thought. I'd heard the word used in so many ways before. Ever since we'd first come it was the word we heard more than any other. When we'd meet them for the first time, they'd say *koneo,* or after an absence, *koneo*—like "hello." Or, when we'd leave for an extended time, *koneo.* If Carol or I or one of the children would fall in the mud on a steep slope they'd be quick to jump down and help, saying, "*Noó, koneo.*"

It seemed to have so many uses I wasn't sure what it meant any more. With some things the closer you look, the more imprecise they are.

Carol had been thinking about it too, and had begun to conclude *koneo* was very possibly the word for "love." It started when she had been visiting the jovial old woman across the way. She'd always tell Carol about her children and her first husband. Her children were grown by then, and her first husband was dead. The enemies had killed him. She'd had more children than were alive, too. A couple of them she hadn't wanted and had strangled them at birth. And when the first husband died, it wasn't too hard, as she never liked him that much anyway. He had been chosen for her and it wasn't much of a match. The second one, however, was much better. He was a widower and she was a widow and they had gotten together.

"I married that one for *koneo*," she said.

Carol had told me about that. Was *koneo* the word for love? We couldn't be sure—not yet; maybe she'd only married him because he was alone; maybe she felt sorry for him. She did say that she was happy, though. So maybe it was love.

That's how it is with language learning—always getting little bits. We'd kept it on file in our heads.

But now, with this story of the younger brother saying *koneo* with his last words. Was it just "goodbye"? Was it "love," like the salutation at the end of a letter? Or was it something deeper, adapting to the relationship and the intensity of the moment?

Hapele and I got back to the business of the verse before us. We went over the whole context again, trying to get its great meaning into Folopa. We'd been struggling. So far I hadn't had much call for the word love. When we had encountered it before, we'd worked around it in other ways—but the deepest significance was never needed in any of those places. Not like it was here.

"For God so loved . . ."

Both of us were in the dark.

Finally I said, "Hapele, would it work if we used the word *koneo* for where God cares so much for the world that He sent His Son?"

Suddenly, the lights went on. "Yes," he said, "that's exactly the right word."

We translated the verse—working it over and over until it made all the right sense.

I was satisfied and impressed once again by how I had been given the words for which I was searching—and without which we could not move on. And it was another case of my thinking I was "taking time off" to relate with the people, this time doing something as far afield as bat hunting in a cave. Yet out of that experience I acquired three new words—each deeply significant.

Legend. Perish. Love.

The word for "legend" became a key that opened door after door into the mysteries of the culture.

"Perish" is a word meaning more than just death. Where else would I have found it but in the legend of Sowé? I had to have it in order to translate this verse—it's as central to the verse as the verse is central to the Bible. As somebody has said, "The good news has to be bad news before it can be good news." Perish is the bad news.

The good news is *koneo*—the deepest love. The deepest *koneo* that a man can give is laying his life down for his friends. The deepest *koneo* that God could give was His Son. It was a sacrifice that would offset the strongest of forces that pull man down.

The telling of it was worth our very lives.

Bind the Strong Man

(Mark 3)

Something woke me up in the middle of the night.

It wasn't that loud or that close, but there was a strangeness about it that brought bumps to my skin. Carol's, too. Aware of every shadow, every dark corner in the house, I got up and went outside.

It was a black night with no moon; just a few stars. The eerie sound—a high-pitched inhuman chant—was coming from the men's house⁵ up the hill. I listened but couldn't get any of the words. I looked for signs of anyone's fire but saw nothing. There was only the shroud of a spine-chilling presence, some evil that pervaded that voice.

I shuddered, prayed for the Lord's protection, and went back to bed.

We'd just been back from furlough for a couple of weeks. Carol had been sensing a stronger than usual need for prayer for the Folopa people, especially in the spiritual dimension. We'd talked about it a number of times. Now I was really beginning to see it, too.

The next day I saw the shaman. He wasn't a regular resident of Fukutao but lived in another village across another mountain. Ironically, though he was reputed to be "the healer," it was his village that was almost gone—decimated by disease. I'd seen the men's house there. It was in a terrible state of disrepair—almost ready to fall down for lack of living male inhabitants.

"Was that you last night?" I asked.

"Yes."

"What were you doing?"

He mumbled something I didn't get. It wouldn't have mattered. He is not a man whose word one could trust. Later on I found out what it had been.

It was Owarape Ali's knee. Owarape Ali was the old fight chief. The one who was so nonplused by our desire to come to the village. He'd had a problem with his knee for a long time and always walked around with a stick. I had treated it when asked. I'd gotten advice from a doctor and given him injections of antibiotics. But he didn't come regularly for the treatment so it never did any good. Since then we have given most of our medicines over to the village people along with some training. They are the ones that need to be taking care of these things and are showing themselves capable in most areas.

A few days later I saw Owarape Ali. He came up leaning on his stick. I nodded at his knee. "Any better?" I asked.

He wagged his head.

"Did it cost you a pig?"

Owarape Ali just grunted and limped off.

The pig is a sacrifice. More than anything the intention is to trick the spirit that's causing the malady. As the pig is slaughtered, its blood and fat are offered to the spirit which, deceived, is satisfied in its desire for a human soul. The rest of the pig goes to the shaman in payment.

We'd begun translating the book of Mark. We were up to the third chapter. Jesus had gone into a synagogue and was stopped by a man with a shriveled hand. Knowing everybody was watching, particularly the religious leaders to catch him working on the Sabbath, He commanded the man to stretch out his hand. As he did so, it was completely restored. No chanting, no high-pitched appeals in the middle of the night, no foreboding presence of the power of darkness, and no slaughtered pig. But as effortless as it had been, the Pharisees didn't like it and plotted to kill Jesus. They charged, "He is possessed by Beelzebub! By the prince of demons he is driving out demons" (Mark 3:22b).

This wasn't even reasonable. Jesus answered, "How can Satan drive out Satan? If a kingdom is divided against itself, that kingdom cannot stand" (Mark 3:23-24).

We kept translating.

And if Satan opposes himself and is divided, he cannot stand; his end has come. In fact, no one can enter a strong man's house and carry off his possessions unless he first ties up the strong man. Then he can rob his house (Mark 3:26-27).

Now there was an analogy I thought would fit Folopa

culture perfectly—a raid. But I was wrong. When we'd gotten the words down and I looked, there was no flicker of understanding in their eyes.

"What is it talking about?" they asked.

"Jesus is talking about Himself here," I explained. "He's coming to get what was rightfully His in the first place. A strong man has taken His possessions and he'll keep them until Jesus, the stronger man, comes. He has got to bind up the one in control of the house before He can take back His possessions."

"Humm," they said, but they still weren't getting it.

"In your fighting days," I asked, "didn't you ever tie people up to steal their goods?"

"No," they said. "We took things but that was never why we went. We always went to kill!"

I could see this was going to be hard. They didn't disarm to rob. That was a foreign concept. The only disarming they knew was dismembering.

Though stealing and petty theft is widespread in these areas, no Folopa would ever tie up another Folopa to steal his goods—regardless of who owned them first. Around here everybody knows everybody else and if he left his victim alive he would always know that he had revenge coming just as soon as the tied-up man told his clan brothers. We needed another metaphor.

Then Awiame Ali said, "It's like with pythons."

"Pythons?"

"Yes, like when we catch them."

"What do you mean?"

"A python is dangerous," he said, "and very strong. When it catches a wild pig it will break every bone in its body. When we hunt them, in order to get them under control we have to bind them first."

Talking about snakes is not uncommon in this area. The Folopa are not repulsed by snakes as we tend to be. Yet they do identify them with evil in all legends and myths. But the truth is, pythons fear the Folopa more than the Folopa fear pythons, and the snakes keep a good distance from the village. The Folopa hunt them for food. Around here, pythons grow to be ten to fifteen feet long and sometimes eighteen inches around. It's enough to make a meal for a whole family with all the relatives.

Hunting python for a feast means taking them alive. Out here there's no refrigeration, no preserving, and once the snake's dead the meat goes bad fast. The only way to keep the meat fresh is to keep it alive.

Hunting python is something of a contest for a Folopa. It's a game, and all the more exciting because the stakes are high. They love to talk about past hunts and recount old stories. Especially the close calls.

"The python will break your bones," Awiame Ali went on. "His teeth are sharp like hundreds of needles all pointing back down his throat. If you get your hand in there there's no getting it out again—he'd rip it off first.

"He's smart, too. He knows the way of the forest. He knows all the trails of the other animals, the tree kangaroos, the wallabies, and where they go to get water at night. He waits, perfectly still, with his mouth open, hiding. When the animal comes by, he strikes. He clamps down on it with his teeth, wrapping his coils around and squeezing until the bones crush. Then, once the prey is dead, the snake leaves it there and goes off to get water which he drinks until he's bloated. Coming back, he has to keep head and tail up so as not to lose the water. Then he vomits it all out over the dead animal, making it slippery so he can swallow it without choking.

"Sometimes we come across one of these dead animals while the python's getting his water. You can always tell an animal that's been killed by a python. It isn't just dead, it has a different shape. So we check which way he went and wait. When he comes back and gets the animal about half-way down his throat, we take him. We get two at once that way."

I leaned back and listened, enjoying it as Awiame Ali continued, but still waiting for how all this connected with "binding the strong man." The others seemed to know.

"Usually we hunt during the day," he said, "when the pythons are sleeping. We watch for their droppings. We keep an eye out up in the trees as well as along the ground where they sleep, all wrapped up with their heads tucked down under their coils. When we know we're getting near, we put some leaves in the back of our belt like this." He showed me, though he didn't need to—I'd been on some python hunts just as an observer. "And we carry some turns of small vine in our teeth. When we see him sleeping we come up on him very quietly. Then we go like this. . . ." He made a clicking sound with his fingernails. "He thinks that's the sound of an animal stepping on twigs and he raises his head up out of his coils to look.

"Right at that precise moment we grab him." Awiame Ali made a lightning jab in the air to show me. "If you miss, that's it. When we get him the fight is on. Coils go flying, looping, trying to get around the hunter.

"That's when you've got to get the leaves on him quick." Awiame Ali whipped out the imaginary leaves from behind his back and clamped them over the imaginary python head in his grip. Then he went through the motions of taking a vine from his mouth, winding it around and around the head, tying the leaves on tight.

Everybody was greatly enjoying the pantomime—easier here with no snake and danger.

"Do you ever miss?" I asked.

"One time Isa got it," he said. "He was up in a tree stalking a snake and the rest of us were a little ways away. When Isa grabbed the neck he didn't get the leaves on in time. The snake got the advantage; the big loops came over him and started to squeeze. It had him by the neck and the power closed in on Isa so fast he didn't have a chance to yell. He had no voice, he was being choked. But he did the right thing. With his remaining strength and the little time he had, he got down out of the tree and ran over to us. It took three of us to pull the snake off of him."

"Did you kill that snake?" I asked.

"No, not right then. We finally got a leaf over its head and tied it on. Once you do that it's over; the snake doesn't know what's up. It's like he loses his power and you can handle him with ease. Then we wrap him around a stick and carry him back."

I've seen them do this. They take a tree branch cut like a large Y with a short post. They tie the tail to the base with vine—so tight it just about cuts off circulation. Then they wrap the snake back and forth up the Y in a series of figure eights. At the top they tie off the head to one side.

As menacing as that snake was a few moments before,

it's then a helpless worm. The strong man is bound. They hoist it over their shoulders and carry it home. When they get it there, and when they are ready to make it into a meal, they take the butt end of an ax and crush its head.

The men in the Bible house had been relishing all this talk. They love anything about danger. But besides that, it was making the passage we were working on a good deal clearer. The Folopa don't bind other men—that didn't make sense—but they do bind pythons. It's a contest, a very dangerous contest, against a very strong opponent— but it's one they always intend to win. And they win by binding it and rendering it helpless.

Any connection between the prince of demons in the passage and the serpent the Folopa thought of to understand the meaning was purely coincidental. Or was it?

Certainly there were, and still are, many in that land still held down by strong and sinister powers. Still, every now and again, we hear the eerie wailing chant in the night. And when we do, our blood still runs cold.

But for the Folopa, a stronger force has come. And He will bind His foe.

12

Whom to Fear

(Luke 12)

Meanwhile, when a crowd of many thousands had gathered, so that they were trampling on one another, Jesus began to speak first to his disciples, saying: "Be on your guard against the yeast of the Pharisees, which is hypocrisy" (Luke 12:1).

We weren't an innumerable multitude, but as we translated Luke, a pretty fair number were coming to the working sessions.

We were on chapter 12. "Be on your guard. . . ." As we mulled the expression over, getting it down accurately, there was a stirring among the listeners on the floor. Being on guard was something these men could relate to—especially the older ones. As we translated the next verse their guard seemed to even increase. They were frightened as Jesus said,

"There is nothing concealed that will not be disclosed, or hidden that will not be made known" (Luke 12:2).

There were two older men who came to the Bible house in those days. They were in their traditional bark capes, arm bands, and big shell earrings. Never having accustomed themselves to chairs or benches, they preferred to sit on the floor, cross-legged. Always listening, they'd busy themselves finding lice in their hair or beards and occasionally making comments about what we were translating or how it related to their view of life. Sometimes they'd silence the younger ones with insights from their years.

These two men were particularly close to me. In my presence the villagers referred to them as my "fathers." One of them had "listened to the Talk" and was a Christian; the other was not. Either way, they loved to hear stories and were especially captivated by those that contained elements of danger. When we'd hit on a passage that would evoke any kind of fear, these old ones would stop their idle activities, look up and say, "I'm afraid."

When the old men said that, everyone knew the impact of the passage had really hit home. Stirred as they were, that didn't necessarily mean they would do anything about it. They had grown up rather used to fear.

The older ones had lived most of their lives during what they called "the fighting days." Often they'd talk about the old battles. Those times finally culminated early in the 1960s when the Australians came in and forcefully put it all to a stop. It wasn't that long ago. I was in college during those years, astronauts were going to the moon, and America was struggling with Vietnam. But out here in Papua New Guinea, Fukutao was fighting its final open wars with its neighbors in the village of Setẹ and did not yet know there was another world beyond, or any escape from their endless cycle of warfare.

It was Awiame Ali who told me about that battle. At that time he was at the height of his youthful vigor.

"It started when someone suddenly died in Fukutao," he said. "He had just returned from a lone trip to the forest; he suffered nausea the following day, mortal sickness the next, then on the third day he died. All the evidence indicated he died from stone magic."

"What is stone magic?" I asked.

He said, "People did stone magic by preparing a wand with a decorated 'incantation stone' wrapped in a piece of split rattan. They would take it outside and wave it in the wind, praying to the ghost of a clan brother—whoever it is they wished to avenge. If there is a response of thunder that is the day for the murder.

"Maybe three of them go out and wait in ambush—one chewing a leaf of a *hilipili* tree and chanting quietly. With magic incantation he makes himself invisible, and with further chants he draws the enemy out of his village and down the trail alone. When he comes, the other two jump out and hack their victim to death. Then the invisible one waves his wand over the body which magically sucks up all the spilled blood and restores the victim to apparent wholeness. He then talks to the corpse: 'Today you will go back to your village feeling well,' he says. 'Tomorrow you will be sick, the next day you will be dying, and on the third you will really die.' Then he rubs a sting nettle leaf on the dead face and the life comes back to the man."

"You mean the life *apparently* comes back to the man."

"Yes," Awiame Ali said, "It comes back to him. Because

he had been sorcerized, the victim has no memory of any of it. He sees the two men, knows they are strangers, but helps them escape, directing them to the best route away from this enemy territory. Then he returns to the village. In four days he's dead."

"That's what happened to the man from Fukutao?"

"Yes, the villagers watched him die and couldn't do anything. During his last moments, the elders gathered around trying to get answers out of him as to who was the murderer. He died without saying anything, which further proved it was sorcery.

"They went into action. They had to have the answer and they jumped up and down on the floor to jiggle the corpse and get a last word. They took the body and shook it, trying to force out the last of the lung air to make some sound in the mouth. Any word can give a clue but in this case nothing happened. So one of the elders held a stick over the corpse and chanted, 'Who did it? Who did it?' As the stick moved, the direction it took indicated the guilty village. The stick pointed toward Setę.

"A little later some of the men came across a small raiding party from Setę—out for murder. We chased them through the bush but they got away. That's when we really prepared for battle.

"We went over there and camped a couple of hours from Setę. We were going to get up in the middle of the night and set an ambush by daybreak, but a Setę scout spotted our cooking fire before we slept. He alerted Setę warriors and before we knew it they sprang on us! We lost a number of men that night and others were wounded.[4]

"We had been beaten and it took months to recover. The

whole time our need for revenge was seething and growing to full force. We determined to eat the whole village of Setę We vowed this time to do it right, to leave nothing.

"When the day came all the men of the village joined in. We painted ourselves up to kill—our faces covered with charcoal highlighted with white lime, the sides of our noses smeared with red dye, bands of beads on our heads, tall black cassowary feathers in our hair, arm bands on our biceps, a big shell over our chests, and pig tusks through our noses. We dressed to weaken the hearts of our enemies with terror; we dressed to kill.

"Those who had killed before wore the special distinction of red *do* 'victory leaves'. These brought relief to suffering widows and earned special status in the village. All night we marched up and down, chanting, rousing ourselves. Again we crept over to the edge of Setę. Everyone had his bone dagger in his arm band and an axe in his belt. Some carried battle axes (saucer-shaped stones, honed all around, good for cleaving heads). Some had bows and arrows and wore their thick bark-cloth shields. Some carried spears. At the first light of dawn we had Setę surrounded. Then one of our warriors was discovered and the battle was on. This time, though, we had the advantage. We swept down on Setę, killing everything in sight—men, women, children, pigs, dogs.

"It was gruesome. About half the people escaped, later showing up in Woposale. The rest were all killed. Before we finished we plundered the place for valuables like axes and beads. Then we burned all the houses, destroyed the gardens; we even chopped down the trees. We dismembered all the bodies, quartering them to carry on the march back. These we cooked and served to mourners at a feast in Fukutao."

When Awiame Ali finished he just looked at me—no doubt trying to discern my blank expression. I had heard these kinds of stories before and had seen how fierce the men can look dressed up in their battle garb as they still like to do for festivities.

"It was terrible," he said. "I can't believe we did all that."

He continued. "With the score settled, we didn't need to go out and kill again—at least not in that direction. We only had to be on guard lest Setę regain strength, or Woposale take up their cause and seek revenge. It could happen to anybody, anytime."

Such was the way of life, and death, for centuries in Papua New Guinea. It kept populations down, the groups scattered and isolated. Without communication between peoples, languages continued to diverge from common roots.

Revenge never came to Fukutao. The Australians came after that, and though they came without facepaint or battle ornaments, they caused more fright among the Folopa than they had known yet. Awiame Ali once told me about that, too.

"When the first two government patrolmen trekked into Fukutao," he said, "everyone ran for the bush. We thought we were seeing ghosts. They were white, not normal at all, and looked like ashen specters from the nether world. We thought they were dead ancestors come back to haunt us, to maim and eat us.

"The whites came heading a column of fifty carriers and national policemen with carbines. They, at least, were black, yet they wore odd clothes—not of bark. But the two white ones in front held the dread. Their hair was moss; their faces, arms, and legs colorless and ghastly. Their feet were brown and their toes seemed to be sewn together. We had never seen shoes or shoelaces.

"As the newcomers settled in the village for the night, they let it be known that they were indeed to be feared. Through interpreters they proclaimed how there was now a new law in the land. War and killing would no longer be tolerated. Neither would taking bones from corpses or any eating of the dead. From then on bodies would be buried, underground, within two days' time, or else! Jail, a cage far away from kinsmen and clan, was waiting for those who ignored these laws.

"To make their point the outsiders bought a pig from the village. In front of everyone they tied it to a stake fifty yards away, took their rifles, and opened fire. People hid in terror at the sound. The pig lay dead, splattered with holes. The Australians instructed the villagers to butcher the pig and see what kind of damage their 'bows' could do."

From that point, all cannibalism and revenge warfare abruptly stopped. That was the end of the fighting days but the memory of that life is still alive, especially in the minds of the old ones. People know there is a final pay-back coming. The new law of the land may have stopped it on one level but there is more to it than that.

Back at the translation table, the Pharisees and teachers of the law were still opposing Jesus, trying to catch Him in something He might say. "Be on guard against the yeast of the Pharisees," he told his followers. In other words, "Don't be hypocritical. Don't talk one way and live another. It all comes out in the end."

The two old men they call my fathers looked up hard. It was always the warnings in Scripture that grabbed their minds the most and froze them cross-legged on the floor. We translated on.

> "What you have said in the dark will be heard in the daylight, and what you have whispered in the ear in the inner rooms will be proclaimed from the house-tops" (Luke 12:3).

"I'm afraid," the one said.

"You should be afraid," the other grunted back. "You're old. You'll die soon. You don't listen to the Talk. What will it be for you?"

The first one shivered. His glance went to the corners of the ceiling and he said nothing more.

Though the overt killing by raid is gone, sorcery is still around. Much of the old mindset still persists. Revenge as a way of life is hard to kill. In fact, except for the occasional obvious murders, all deaths are still attributed to sorcery. The proof is simple. If a person falls ill but recovers, he was only sick—but if he dies, he was sorcerized.

Fear, the constant companion of the Folopa and the motivation for almost every daily action for generations, still persists as the basic outlook among many—even with the new law in the land.

Even the believers aren't sure about sorcery. They've lived with it all too long. They've seen a lot of people die strange deaths. They know there's a power out there. Whether or not it's the cause of all death remains a question for them. But they aren't without hope. They figure whatever death's cause, heaven is waiting. Whatever agent God wants to use to get them there is in His hands. It's a comfort they didn't have before.

We translated the next verse. "I tell you, my friends, do not be afraid of those who kill the body and after that can do no more" (12:4).

At that point one of the old men, the one who listens to the Talk, spoke up. "There's nothing to fear," he said. The rest of the men looked at him, but he was quiet again and we translated on. "But I will show you whom you should fear: Fear him who, after the killing of the body, has power to throw you into hell. Yes, I tell you, fear him" (Luke 12:5).

The same old one looked up again from his place on the floor. "We fear God," he said, putting his hand to his throat in the classic Folopa manner of expressing most somber truths. "And the fear of God kills our fear of everything else. This," he said, "is a great *beté*."

13

Don't Say a Prayer

We were working on prayer. Not that prayer isn't always work—but this time we were grappling with the deeper concepts of what prayer means, both to us and the Folopa.

David Hynum had come up from another part of the country to help us with some checking. It's all part of the process we go though to ensure that newly translated scriptures are communicating accurately. David is a linguist and Bible translator in another Papua New Guinean language. Though he doesn't know Folopa, he knows Pidgin as do a few of the men of the village. With that they were able to dialogue with enough depth to satisfy the situation of the moment.

Actually we worked with an English "back translation" that Carol and I produced to show what was literally there in Folopa. Following along as the men read in Folopa, David would stop and ask the meaning of certain terms. The process is called key term checking and is an effective way of getting at real understanding. At a certain verse he stopped and asked for more explanation for *hosǫ* 'prayer'.

Hosǫ is the word they'd been using since the days of Kirapareke, when he came and introduced the concept in the first place. It was an old word even if it was a new concept. Before they knew the Lord, of course, there was no one to pray to—but when they needed a term they'd taken the closest equivalent they could come up with at the time.

The truth is, I wondered about it when we'd first addressed it at the translation table. From what I knew of the original meaning, *hosǫ* seemed to have more to do with some sort of incantation, and I questioned whether this was the right term for the Christian concept of prayer. I'd even suggested that we might use another word I'd heard, *moma.* But they had discarded that as too closely associated with contacting spirits, so we let it go. Besides, by then they were used to using *hosǫ,* and words take on new meanings in time in any case.

But David kept probing. Roots of words are significant, and he wanted to get to the bottom of this one.

He asked them, "How did you use this word before you started using it as prayer to God?"

"We used to use it to plant our gardens," they said, "or to hunt."

"How did you do *hosǫ*?" David asked.

"Different ways," they said, "depending on the situation. But whenever we did it, we had to do it just right."

"Meaning what?"

"Well," they went on, "when we wanted a pig to grow up big and healthy we would put our mouth down close to the back of the pig's neck and ears and repeat the sayings."

"You had a certain form of speech?"

"Yes. You had to do it just right and keep saying the same things over."

"How else did you use it?"

"Many ways. We did it for every stage of our planting, starting with our garden fences. If you don't make a good fence to keep pigs out they will get in and eat everything before we do. To build a fence right we would wrap our axe handles with a certain kind of leaf and say a specific *hosọ* over it before building it. Then as we prepared the soil we had another special saying. We did the same when we planted yams or whatever we were putting in the ground. Later when the first shoot would come up we would get down close to it and say a *hosọ*. As we would insert a pole in the ground to give the vine something to climb we tied it with a special leaf and said another *hosọ*. As the plant would grow we had another *hosọ* to protect the *beté* underground where beetles and insects might well come and eat it before time for harvest."

"Did it work?" David asked.

"Who knows?" they answered. "People always did it. It was the only way."

"Do some people still do it?" David asked.

"Some do," they said, "others pray."

But as they said this they used the same word, *hosọ*. It was only the certain inflection of voice, the focused look, the you-know-what-I-mean nod that conveyed another meaning. Such distinctives might work in oral communication, but one doesn't have those in print and more precision might well be called for. That's what David was getting at.

"How else did you use this word?" he asked.

"In our hunting," they said.

"How?"

"Different ways, depending on what we were hunting, or if we were using traps."

"For instance?"

"If we were using traps, we would say a *hosǫ* as we made them, whether twitch-up traps, or noose traps, or dead-fall traps. Then we'd want the human scent to go away so the animal would come put his head in so we'd say a *hosǫ* to make it rain."

"Did it work?" David was aware of the humor of his question. It rains every day three quarters of the year in this part of the country.

They laughed with his smile. "Of course it worked."

"And did it work on the traps?"

"Traps always work," they said, ". . . eventually."

"How about when hunting with bow and arrow?"

"We did *hosǫ* then, too. First we'd find where the animals are—the wild pigs, cassowary, tree kangaroos, or *cuscus.* They're all creatures of habit and leave trails or markings at the bottoms of trees, or whatever. So we could just watch their trails, but we don't want to sit there forever, always ready and not knowing when they're going to come. Besides, when they do come they may go by so fast you can't get a shot. For that we set an ambush."

"How?"

"We break a little stick off and put it in his trail. Then when he comes by he notices something new, something with a new scent, and as he hesitates ever so briefly it's enough to get a shot."

"And to keep from having to wait forever you'd use *hoso*."

"Yes."

"Do you still?"

"Some do, but some use *hoso*," they said with a nod and there we were again. The men were beginning to see what David was driving at.

David asked me if there was another word and I told him about *moma*. David began probing into that area. As he went he began to see something of their old hesitation to use that word, yet it really seemed to fit more precisely with the real meaning of prayer.

Moma, in years past, was something of a speech addressed to the powerful spiritual beings, particularly the spirits of departed people. It wasn't an incantation or a matter of "method," but was something more spontaneous and adaptable to the situation and the desire sought. Christians, however, had been repulsed by the term, not because of its activity as a verb, but because of the noun to whom it was addressed.

"What is the bottom-line power of the two concepts?" David asked.

"The *beté* of *hoso* is in the words and in saying them just right," they replied. "The *beté* of *moma* is different: it's in the power of the spirit to whom it is addressed."

"The latter sounds more like the real prayer you do when you pray to the Father. Is that so?"

They hadn't thought of it that way yet. There were reasons. Their tradition of using spiritual communication had only been focused on wrong spirits because in the past wrong spirits were all they knew.

But now they knew that God also is Spirit, and He is worshiped in spirit and truth. Truth is from the heart and the mind, and not encapsulated in some rote incantation.

As David and I talked about it later we reflected on how there are those in the world who pray to Satan. But that shouldn't deter those who love God from using the word *prayer* or from enjoying its power.

Nevertheless, certain words *are* powerful and carry strong associations and meanings. How many in our own culture and language mean something very different by the word prayer than God intended when He provided that means of communication with Himself? How often do moderns still "say a prayer," using some memorized or rote approach, thinking (or not thinking at all) that by this they are doing all that can be done to get through to God?

We had been learning some deeper things about prayer ourselves in those days. Not that we hadn't depended on prayer all along—or rather on the God who answers prayer—but not long after our family had first come to the village we had cause for a deeper experience of its power.

In those days our children were having terrible nightmares. Heather and Dan would wake up in the middle of the night in terror, so frightened they could hardly cry. Nor could they explain exactly the visions they were seeing, at least not in any coherence to us who tried our best to comfort them. At first, though we were concerned when it would happen, we thought little of it, knowing that children go through these things. We would tell them nothing was there, that nothing would hurt them. But we could not go far before they would call out again.

It persisted. Of course we would pray with them, that they would not be afraid. That bolstered their courage some, but still the dreams kept coming. Finally Carol began to sense that this was some real oppression that we were up against, and that it was attacking us at our weakest point—our children.

She remembered some friends in Africa who had experienced this same thing and how they had begun to pray in a much more direct way, commanding the spirits to leave. So we adopted the same approach. When Heather or Dan would cry out in the night we would come and rebuke the devil, commanding the spirits to depart, and we would ask the Lord Jesus to come and stand at their bedside for the duration of the night. We found that when we did this the children would return to sleep for the rest of the night undisturbed.

In time we were doing this every night, finally adopting the habit of doing it before bed, before anything might happen. We had always prayed with our children before bed, but not at this level. Stronger measures were now called for. As we persisted in this, the problem with the nightmares went away.

Our own concept of prayer deepened in those days. And in truth, who of us does not have much to learn in that area? It starts with a relationship, of knowing who God is and what He has promised, and it grows with a sense of need, of what we're up against in daily living, particularly in the spiritual realm.

But part of it starts with having a concept of what prayer is in the first place. For the Folopa, it all began to deepen when they started labeling prayer by a term that's closer to its real meaning. The power is in the one addressed, not the particular way it's said.

14

He Is the Father, and He Is Good

(Luke 11)

We were translating Luke 11 and one of the disciples asked Jesus to teach them to pray. Starting out with the word "Father," He gave them what has become the most famous of prayers, and perhaps the outline for all prayer.

As we were working through it, an old man and a child knocked at the door. The Bible house was already full but they came in and some squeezed closer together to give them a place on the floor. We had more people wanting to come in those days than we could possibly fit. When we started the book, forty men were showing up at the Bible house, which was only twelve feet square.

We had to do something about this crowd so I made a big chart. I wrote down the names of people and which days they could come, taking care that there would always be a nucleus of the sharpest ones coming every day. Restricting it to twelve men per day ensured that we never had more than about sixteen. Some of the older men considered themselves exempt from such rules and would come regardless of the day.

Some just liked the stories. Some of the older ones came because it was the only interesting thing in the village for them to do. They, by reason of seniority, had earned the right to retire from gardening and hunting. Instead, they stayed in the village all day, watching children and generally guarding the place. Others, like Awiame Ali, came because they didn't want to miss anything.

"I'm going to die doing this," he always said.

When they brought children, I tried not to let them get under my skin. They'd be playing around on the floor, under the table, or on top. It got a little distracting at times. Sometimes they were hungry and whiny. Children like to snack but there was nothing to eat in the Bible house. Nor is there ever anything to snack on around a Folopa house during the day. There are no cupboards, no refrigerators, and no packaged foods. The older kids get pretty adept at foraging and any of the younger ones who aren't with their mother in the garden just go hungry until she comes home.

We translated a few more verses and two more children came in—one of them entreating his father for something to eat, the other just then squeezing the life out of a grasshopper and popping it into his mouth.

I tried to ignore all this. We translated Luke 11:9.

Ask and it will be given to you; seek and you will find; knock and the door will be opened to you.

That open door business is good for the kingdom of God, I thought, *but it's getting a little distracting around here! I wish it would stay closed for awhile.*

We moved on. In verse 11 Jesus drew a picture. "Which of you fathers," He said, "if your son asks for a fish, will give him a snake instead?"

As I described it, the men looked at me in surprise. "Why not?" somebody asked.

"Why not *what?*" I asked back.

"Why not give him a snake?"

"Because of God's goodness," I said. "When you ask for something that's good for you, He's not going to give you something that's harmful. You can trust Him. He's a father. He's good."

Among the Folopa and all the cultures of Papua New Guinea, the family relationship is very strong. Parents devote a great deal of time and devotion to their children. They really love them. They're careful to train and mentor them. It's kind of like an apprenticeship. They include them in their lives from the time they can walk. They are never excluded. They are never left behind from parental activities. Little boys, as soon as they can keep up and do their part, are allowed to go hunting. Little girls go on expeditions with their mothers to the bush. The women's specialty is catching a certain kind of field mice and they teach the girls how to do this and how to gather all sorts of morsels.

Consequently then, with all this parental love and care, the idea of God as our Father as He is presented in the Bible fits right into their culture.

God, however, was not pictured as such in Folopa tradition. The Folopa name for God is Boporowae. Boporowae is remote and unconcerned and far removed from a father—certainly not a good father. "If he does anything at all," they say, "we don't know what it is . . . except hold the world down."

"Did he create the world?" I asked once.

"Oh yes, he probably did, but nobody ever gives him much thought. He has no involvement at all in human affairs. The only thing he does now is sit on his haunches over the world, keeping it in place with his elbows. When he gets stiff and needs to stretch, that's when the earth rumbles and quakes. Other than that no one ever hears from him."

The men in the room were all aware that the old views of God as Boporowae were out of date. What they didn't understand was why Jesus would say what He just did.

"Why wouldn't a father who is good give his son a snake instead of a fish?"

To a Folopa, offering a meal of snake is like serving roast turkey at Thanksgiving. They wrap it in a coil like a giant sweet roll and steam it between hot rocks covered with banana leaves. Since in a snake the heart and liver run much of its length, almost every slice will contain a bite of these delicacies.

On the other hand, fish in Folopa territory are very small. They make a meal of no consequence. Each one is just a bite. They're caught in nets or with a scoop or with derris root poison. (The poison is enough to stun the fish and cause them to float to the surface, but the fish meat thus killed is not harmful to humans.) To cook, they stuff them in bamboo tubes and lay them over the fire. But they're a small meal.

As we talked about it, I began to see what they were getting at.

If you then, though you are evil, know how to give good gifts to your children, how much more will your Father in heaven? (Luke 11:13).

Why not give a snake instead of a fish?

The difference, of course, was in the view of snakes and their use between the two cultures. The people to whom Jesus was talking didn't eat snakes. In that society they were considered unclean. They *were* unclean. There was nothing redeeming about them at all. But in *any* culture a good father would never give his son, when he asks for something good, something that could harm him instead. That's a universal truth.

We worked at it awhile longer. Finally we came up with something like: "If your son is hungry and he wants a fish, you wouldn't toss him a live snake of the kind that when it bites people they die."

I looked at it, still not sure that was the perfect translation. But it was as close as we could come for the moment keeping the meaning intact.

The point wasn't the fish or the snake in any case, but the "how much more." God is our Father. How much more than we as fathers is our Heavenly Father likely to be good. He entreats us to make requests of Him and when we do, He is pleased to give us something even better than we asked. Too bad a lot of people in the Western world—even those who have had a Bible a lot longer than the

Folopa—still envision God as the disinterested Boporowae, and never ask anything in His name.

They still haven't learned that He is the Father, and He is good.

15

Who Is My Neighbor?

(Luke 10)

There are seventeen Folopa villages spread out over 1500 square miles of rugged, mountainous jungle. Each of these villages is populated by about three hundred people. Almost exclusively they are perched at the top of steep ridges for defense reasons. Such positions are harder to access. Each village is considered something of a "command center," dominated by its longhouse where the men live. Folopa villages traditionally fought other Folopa villages, though to some extent they warred with villages of other language groups as well. They also had alliances among certain villages, both Folopa and other.

All the societies in Papua New Guinea have long been webbed with well-defined lines of relationship. From infancy everyone is taught who he is related to and what that means—in terms of gifts, future bride price, help, protection, or any other responsibility. Having a sister marry into another clan in another village will extend the relationship bonds where they might not have been before. And that could mean a meal someday, or a place to sleep, or much more.

The divisions between friendly neighbors, known in the Folopa language as *be whị* and enemies, *bóe whị* go back farther than anyone can remember. And though a new law came to the land and put a stop to the wars and raids that would threaten villages as often as every two weeks, centuries-old enmities do not die easily.

There is an airstrip down at Woposale which makes it a place to go from time to time, to pick up some rice that's come in by plane or some canned fish or cloth—things to stock their small trade store. To reach Woposale is a full day's walk on a rugged and steep trail, but Fukutao men do not like to spend the night there. Woposale was an enemy village, and the ally to which the remnant of Setẹ fled when Fukutao men wiped it out, just before government intervention. Now if the men from Fukutao find themselves in a situation where they do have to stay overnight, they always seek housing with the pastor.

Sometimes men of Fukutao will go over to Erave, maybe to sell a cassowary to those who treasure the feathers. It's a three-day trek and to get there they have to pass through the territories of two different language groups, Samberigi and Pole. The first couple of villages they have to pass through were traditional enemies. They have some allies in the next. When they reach Erave they don't know what they will find.

Erave is a district center. It has an airstrip, a clinic, and a large trade store. Consequently it is a gathering place for people from villages all around the area—some of whom will be old enemies. Of course with government control there, outward trouble is generally kept to a minimum, but the threat of sorcery still looms. Visitors are left with locating allies and staying with them and doing their best to avoid contact with their enemies. When the Lord said, "You have heard that it was said, 'Love your neighbor and hate your enemy'" in Matthew 5:43, these people would have been in hearty agreement. But when he said, "But I tell you: Love your enemies," well, that's fairly revolutionary—just as much for the Folopa as for anybody.

Once I was reprimanded for showing kindness to a pair of traditional enemies, though I didn't know it (and of course wouldn't have acted any differently if I had).

Some outsiders passed through Fukutao and came to our house to ask for matches. People that live in these parts hardly ever need matches. Cooking fires burn continually in the villages. At least deep embers can always be restored. The only time a person might need matches is when he plans to spend the night in the forest. Even then he can make a fire without a match, but with matches it's less work. I didn't think of it at the time, but later I realized that the very fact that these men had asked me for matches was their tacit acknowledgment that they would be spending the night in the forest—they knew they could not expect any hospitality in Fukutao.

I gave them the matches. It was noted around the village and later one of the old men told me that I should not have given matches to them. When I asked why not, he said the men were from Hala. Hala was an old enemy village.

This was the environment we were in when we came to translate Luke 10 and the story of the good Samaritan.

That proved a formidable passage to struggle through. Though it starts out easy enough, being a simple dialogue between an expert in the law and Jesus, before long we found ourselves in a morass of difficulties and confusion.

> On one occasion an expert in the law stood up to test Jesus. "Teacher," he asked, "what must I do to inherit eternal life?" "What is written in the Law?" He replied. "How do you read it?" He answered: " 'Love the Lord your God with all your heart and with all your soul and with all your strength and with all your mind;' and, 'Love your neighbor as yourself.' " "You have answered correctly," Jesus replied. "Do this and you will live." But he wanted to justify himself, so he asked Jesus, "And who is my neighbor?" (Luke 10:25-29).

Up to this point we were doing fine translating the dialogue. Here, however, as Jesus started His story, I should have made it more clear that we were going into a story within a story. It can be a subtle feature but every language has some way of signaling changes in levels of discourse— like when the subject changes or one story finishes and another begins. In English or Greek, the context will most often suffice (though even then we can experience confusion). In Folopa, however, it must be explicit. But the first time through we missed it.

Translating on, then:

> In reply Jesus said: "A man was going down from Jerusalem to Jericho, when he fell into the hands of robbers. They stripped him of his clothes, beat him and went away, leaving him half dead."

We had already gone over the fact that in other cultures people would sometimes be robbed and not killed.

A priest happened to be going down the same road, and when he saw the man, he passed by on the other side.

Around these parts roads are almost unknown but there are paths, and though in their mind's eye those at the table likely envisioned something quite narrow with the priest having to make some effort to get around the robbed victim, it still worked.

So, too, a Levite, when he came to the place and saw him, passed by on the other side.

We had discussed Levites before, members of a clan with special religious distinction and function.

But a Samaritan, as he traveled, came where the man was; and when he saw him, he took pity on him.

Now we had to stop and talk about what a Samaritan was, a citizen of neighboring Samaria—and about the enmity that had existed between these two groups for a very long time.

He went to him and bandaged his wounds, pouring on oil and wine.

Suddenly we were stuck. I knew no word for wounds and I had a difficult time getting one. I said, "The word is for things like sores, but they're not sores; it's like injuries, but not accidental."

They were trying to grasp it. "Read it again," they said. So I read it again, explaining as I went.

"These thieves had jumped him," I said, "and he's down, and now he's lying there with these . . . problems . . . these results of what was perpetrated upon him. But what's the word?"

"What did they use on him?"

"I don't know what they used on him. What does it matter?"

"We have to know what they used on him or we can't tell you the word."

"Why not?"

"Because it all depends. If he was speared we say, 'where the spear stood;' if he was shot with an arrow we say, 'where the arrow stood;' if he was axed we say, 'where the axe stood.' You tell us what they used on him and we'll tell you how to say it."

Apparently there was no generic word for "wounds" and this was the best we were going to do. The only trouble was, Scripture didn't tell how it happened. In the original telling, it wasn't important.

So we tried to figure it out.

"Let's say it was a spear," I said.

"Okay," the old ones said, the ones with the most experience with this kind of thing, "did the man live?"

"Yes, he lived," I said.

"Then it wasn't a spear. If it was a spear he would have most likely died."

"Maybe it was an arrow," I offered.

"No, if it had been by arrows they would have pulled them out. Does it say anything about pulling arrows out?"

"No. What about a dagger?"

"No," they said, "if it had been a dagger he probably would have never recovered either."

"Then what about an ax?"

"No way. If they had axed him that would have been the end of him right then!"

"Well then, maybe they just beat him up with their hands," I said.

"No," they protested, "when you do that the person may be covered with lumps and bumps but there's nothing open, nothing for the Samaritan to pour medicine into."

"Then you tell me," I said.

"Well, he was lying there on the road, half dead, bleeding but still alive. He must have been beaten with clubs." With general agreement on that I wrote it down: *nópulu daayale tiki* 'where the clubs stood'. We were off and moving again.

Then he put the man on his own donkey, took him to an inn and took care of him. The next day he took out two silver coins and gave them to the innkeeper. "Look after him," he said, "and when I return, I will reimburse you for any extra expense you may have" (Luke 10:34-35).

That wasn't easy either. As we went on I became aware of that old blank stare in the eyes around me. Something wasn't connecting—again. I realized what it was when I needed the word for inn. In this society there is no such thing. Though hospitality for friends and clansmen is as important and as natural as having breakfast, having a place in the village set aside just for people from out of the area to sleep was a completely foreign idea. And then the idea of *paying* for hospitality, with money, was worlds removed from anything they had ever thought about.

But we had to move on. Without a word for inn, we just had to explain it. I wrote, "a house for sleeping for a person who's on a journey where they have to pay." Not too smooth but what can you do?

We came to the final clincher of the story and translated: "Which of these three do you think was a neighbor to the man who fell into the hands of robbers?"

I looked up at the men, expecting they would answer the question themselves and come up with the same one the law expert was about to, but I was wrong.

Awiame Ali ventured, "The innkeeper?"

When I reacted puzzled, another said, "The expert in the law!"

That's when I realized we had a problem with this discourse-level marker that wasn't there—and needed to be. Jesus was talking about the three characters in His story: the priest, the Levite, and the Samaritan. His story was a subsection of the whole discourse between Jesus and the lawyer, but it took some straightening out of the grammar for everybody to catch it. Then we translated the last verse: "The expert in the law replied, 'The one who had mercy on him.' Jesus told him, 'Go and do likewise.' "

Finally we had it. Finally everybody in the Bible house knew who was saying what to whom and when, what kind of wound it had been, how there was a special place to put guests, and why the Samaritan paid the innkeeper money. The hardest thing now was to follow what had been easiest to translate—that last phrase.

The question the expert in the law asked would have been the same one the folks around here would have hid behind. Maybe we all hide behind it. Who is our *be whị* 'neighbor', and who is our *bóe whį* 'enemy'? Jesus made it clear, our enemy is our neighbor, or more specifically, that one who still considers us his enemy is still that one we are neighborly to.

These are basic yet lofty concepts, and who of us have adopted them as we should? Still I've seen progress among the believers. They move around even among old enemy villages when reasons arise, showing kindness, trusting God. I remember one time when we had finished a draft of the book of Acts and we wanted to check it to see if it was clear. We trekked a long way through Folopa villages where there were no readers and where they had heard very little of the Bible at all. Many of these were old enemy villages. Still, the men in our group showed themselves unafraid and open. They would freely share and read the Scriptures to anyone who would gather.

It would have been very natural to be jittery and leery of any sort of sorcery, yet they were brave and ready to show love to an old enemy.

And that is the *beté* of the gospel.

16

━━◆◈◆━━

Broken Bodies

(Mark 5:7-8; Mark 10:33-34)

Did you ever capture enemies?"

They hesitated. What in the world was I getting at? Why would I want to bring up the past like that?

Of the twelve men in the Bible house, some were of the older vintage. Some were known as "fight chiefs" in their day. Owarape Ali was there, and Eleké Whi Ali̧, men still distinguished as "big men" around the village.

Some in the room had listened to the Talk. A few hadn't—but even they were struck by the qualities of the Man Jesus, His character, His teaching, and His acts.

By the time we reached the fifth chapter, Jesus had gathered disciples, healed the sick, calmed the storm, and generally let His identity be known. Even the spirits gave testimony to who He was.

he Folopa loved the boldness with which Jesus
proached the wild man in the Gerasene tombs. That
han was a beast. No man could subdue him and chains
could not hold him; night and day he would cry out and
cut himself with stones. But the real source of his strength,
not to mention his agony, manifest when he ran up to
Jesus, fell at His feet, and shouted at the top of his voice:

"What do you want with me, Jesus, Son of the Most
High God? Swear to God that you won't torture me!"
For Jesus was saying to him, "Come out of this man,
you evil spirit!" (Mark 5:7-8).

We got to the middle of that verse and could go no further; we did not have a word for "torture." That's when I
asked them if they had ever captured enemies.

They said they had.

I groped further. "When you captured them, did you
ever hit them with sticks or anything like that?"

By this time their eyes were boring holes through me.

Finally Hapele caught on to what I was getting at and
ventured a few descriptions. Soon others, especially the
older ones, joined in with a cascade of graphic descriptions of the worst torture I'd ever heard . . . like the times
they would hold torches up to the captured person's skin
until it blistered, or they'd pour boiling water on him until
the skin literally came off. Or they'd tie him spread eagled
and naked to the ground and have the women beat him
with their digging sticks, concentrating particularly on the
private parts. Or they would tie the enemy to a stake and
with a bamboo knife, cut off a bicep, take it to the fire,
cook it, and return to stand in front of him, taking bites,
saying, "I'm eating your flesh."

Now it was my eyes which bore holes through them.

It was obviously far better to die outright at the hands of these warriors than to be captured, taken back to the village and killed slowly. With the constant revenge killings, there was an abject hatred for the group that had last raided and killed members of their village. Nothing was bad enough.

I was stunned. *Who am I working with?* I thought. All I had done was to explore around a little to find a word and it was like I had turned the key to open the bottomless pit. No wonder they'd reacted as they had when I asked my question. In any case, yes, they did have a word for torture, *susupu eratapó*. And if the demons in Mark 5 had had anything like this in mind—though it was the very stuff they had been instigating in the world down through time—it was no wonder they were afraid.

About a week later we broached the subject again. We'd moved up to Mark 10. This time it wasn't demons fearing torment; rather it was Jesus predicting what was about to happen to Him.

> "We are going up to Jerusalem," he said, "and the Son of Man will be betrayed to the chief priests and teachers of the law. They will condemn him to death and will hand him over to the Gentiles, who will mock him and spit on him, flog him and kill him. Three days later he will rise" (Mark 10:33-34).

Again we were stuck. I didn't have a word for "flog."

"What do you call it," I asked, "if someone hits another, say an enemy, with something like a rope?"

That drew a blank. Apparently hitting someone with a rope was nothing that sounded familiar to them. But it was about to happen to Jesus and it was part of the passage so I cast about for other ways to describe it. My eyes fell on a piece of rattan vine left over from tying the thatch on the roof. It was lying on the old wood-stove. The vine was about three feet long and as thick as my little finger. I went around the table, picked it up, and instructed the men to imagine the vine was a piece of rope and the woodstove was the back of Jesus. Then with all my might I started beating the iron top of the stove.

Immediately Owarape Ali—his eyes wild and his nostrils flaring—shouted out: "That's not hitting with a rope, that's *fokosó sirapó!*" He was indignant, staring up at me from his place on the floor.

Fokosó sirapó. I walked back around the table and wrote the words down.

"Tell me more about it," I said.

But when I looked up they were all just staring at me. It was like it had taken them right back to the old days.

"Wait a minute," someone said. *"Do you mean to say they did THAT to Jesus?"*

"Yes."

"But here He just said they were *going* to do it. Did they really do it to Him?"

"Yes."

Quiet fell on the room. Finally Eleké Whị Ali said, "We used to do that. But we only did it to our enemies, and then just before we were going to kill them."

"Yes," I said, "that is coming, too."

Heads were down. In the corners, the large shell earrings of the old men swung back and forth in utter dejection. The memory of *fokosó sirapó* 'floggings' was too fresh in their minds. They were seeing a deeper vision of the abject cruelty—the enormity of it all—than I had ever considered. And that this would happen to Jesus . . . someone they had grown to respect and like. He was a Man who would put little children on His lap, who would reach out and heal those in need, a Man who could hardly have an enemy. These men knew what torturing and flogging were all about. That this Jesus would come to suffer like this was just too much to take in.

We had to stop for the morning.

17

Crucifixion Pictured

As the crucifixion of Christ is recorded in each of the gospels, we went over the story several times. Each time more details came out. Even I, who have read on it so much, heard so many sermons, seen films, celebrated Easter, and observed the Lord's supper so often, found new things to meditate on—and all the more seeing it afresh through Folopa eyes and language.

In Folopa there is no equivalent for the word crucifixion. Even in English it's a very specialized word meaning just one thing—and that one thing doesn't exist in Folopa culture. Each time we would come to it we found there were more points to clarify from erroneous preconceptions. Though they knew the story since before we ever came to live with them, their perception was skewed in various aspects.

The practice of crucifying is not a part of our culture either but its tradition in history is, particularly because of Christ. We've grown up knowing what crucifixion is: a form of execution by hanging a person up on a large wooden stake or pole, complete with a cross piece for the arms, and leaving him there to suffer until he dies. This had all been new to the Folopa. Even in the long heritage of torture and killing there had never been anything like this, and when they first heard about the crucifixion they misunderstood it. They thought it meant the victim was killed and then hung up on a cross. For years that's what they believed had happened with Jesus until we went through it the first time in the Bible translation process.

For the first time they realized that Jesus talked while He was on the cross. He drank. He prayed. These are activities of a person still living—yet somehow these "incidentals" hadn't come across to them before. In fact, the whole reality of the death, and especially the resurrection, hadn't registered with them much—in spite of their being such central tenets of the message from God about His Son coming to earth for men.

Of course we have to realize that the whole thing was a progressive revelation—both in history and for the Folopa. In the gospels, the crucifixion and the resurrection just happen. Most of the explanation of what it all means comes out later—in Acts or in the epistles. In this regard, the Folopa were coming to it all something like the first eyewitnesses did; seeing, but not yet understanding. The original eyewitnesses, however, at least understood what a crucifixion was. The Folopa had a difficult time visualizing it. Even where Scripture says two thieves were crucified with Jesus, one on the right and one on the left, I had to make it explicit in the text that there were three crosses.

Some of them tended to see Jesus and the two others all hanging together on the same cross.

These cultural gaps of understanding go both ways. Since Carol and I hadn't grown up in Folopa culture, we often wouldn't know when the people were interpreting some biblical event in a completely different way than we were. The concept of resurrection, for example, took a particularly long time to work through. It's another English term for which the Folopa have no literal equivalent. In the gospels the term is not used; the event just happens. Later, the commentary comes through loud and clear—about the empty tomb, the meaning of the bodily resurrection of Jesus, and the promise of the same for all who believe. When these truths finally did hit home, however, they did so with profound effect—much more than we were ever used to seeing in our own culture.

It was something completely new. In the traditional Folopa belief, when a person dies, his spirit leaves his body and lingers around the village for awhile. As it can become either hostile or friendly, it is important to get on its good side. There are various things one does to ensure this. Eventually the spirit moves away from the village and goes to a place called Siki Ao. We've never been able to find out much about this place. The Folopa don't seem to have a clear picture of what it is themselves; just that it is where the spirits go when they've finished their business around the village. The spirits of the recently deceased whose names are still remembered can be called back as they are summoned by shamans. Those who have been forgotten and are consequently nameless cannot be summoned, however.

Siki Ao is a dark area and those who do have knowledge of it don't share it. They would be particularly reticent to share it with those of us who have come with news of another Spirit, and news of resurrection, and bodily resurrection at that—where the believer will be glorified forever in heaven. Their term for heaven is Talene Be, which can be translated either as "the Lord's place" or "the owner's home." The concept of it being a home at all, where they will not be alone but where there is family, love, and light—rather than darkness and solitude and evil—is completely new to them.

All this deeply moved the Folopa as it sank in.

That this is the greatest free gift on the face of the earth can hardly be denied. The fact that for many it *is* too good to believe and they consequently don't is another matter. It is what the Scripture teaches. But it also teaches that, in fact, the gift was not free. There was a price to be paid and, because it was beyond mankind's means to pay it, God did it Himself through the sacrificial death of His Son. The means of execution was extreme, but so was the crime. Jesus paid for the sin of all. In time the Folopa began to see how there was quite a difference between Jesus dying and then being hung on a cross for display and His dying a slow and agonizing death on that cross.

The men involved in the translation process were getting a better grasp of all this, but it was when we got a set of films of the gospel story that it really began to touch the rest of the village. We had a whole set—a dramatic portrayal of the book of Luke. We showed it in the church building every evening for twenty-four nights after we had translated Luke. People crowded in and sat on the floor, the men on one side of the room, the women and children on the other, as is their custom.

They were highly intrigued. Since they weren't familiar

with films at all, we had to keep emphasizing that this was a reenactment of something that happened. The people in the films were not the real people—they were only actors. They were only dressed up to look like the people of a long time ago to give a better idea of what it was like.

Every evening we would read that chapter of Scripture in Folopa and then show the film. The film was not in Folopa so they would have to remember what we just read as they watched the film. It worked pretty well. The parts that they found difficult to understand we would discuss afterward. They were really impressed with things like the feeding of the five thousand or Peter pulling in so many fish that the nets were breaking.

But nothing, nothing, compared with the impact of the crucifixion.

A silence came over the church floor as the soldiers laid Jesus down on the cross. He was still alive; everyone could see that. But that silence was only the calm before the storm. At the first hammer blow on the nail into Jesus' hand all the women in the church erupted into an excruciating wail. It made the scene on the film all the more terrible. The men, sitting on their side, tried to keep the women quiet, but they would not stop.

"It's not real!" they shouted. "That's not really Jesus!" But they were apparently not convinced. It was like Jesus was actually dying right there before them.

It was a culturally appropriate response. In a way, I suppose it was no different than our applause at some heroic event in a movie theater even though the actors are not themselves present. But the whole thing, Jesus being nailed to that wood and then erected high so all could see who was winning and who was losing, seemed more eerie and perhaps more real with the uproarious wailing from the women live in the room. It had a lasting effect on Carol and me.

In the end, beneath the clamor, Jesus mouthed the words which we had read at the beginning, "Father, forgive them, for they do not know what they are doing."

These words, of all, had the most profound effect on those sitting on the floor of the church. Somehow, though in ways none of us truly comprehend, the Father did hear that prayer and did forgive—not only for but by this very act of crucifixion. It was another discovery of *beté*—the root source of all things.

People returned to their huts more somber those evenings. The crucifixion seemed closer to all of us—and our hearts closer to God.

18

Payback

(Luke 22:19-20)

When we first started living in Fukutao, it was only God's grace that protected me from my ignorance. That hasn't changed, but over the years we've learned a few things.

It was very early in our first term when I learned first-hand about payback. We didn't know a lot of what was going on around us yet. We'd done our homework and reading, of course, as part of our orientation. But it's not the same as finding things out by living them.

We were building our house and I was up on the roof. We hadn't put the thatch on yet and I was in the process of cutting one of the rafters that was sticking up too high. People were all around, some watching, some helping, and I called out for someone to hand me an ax. A man from another village, Wei Ali, picked up an ax and handed it to me. As I pulled it up, it caught on something and jerked out of my hand. The ax slid away and went over the edge, falling on and grazing Wei Ali. The skin cut was only slight, thank God, but it had put a good tear in his shirt.

Immediately there was great commotion. People were yelling and shouting, looking at Wei Ali and looking back at me. It was apparent that a terrible thing had just happened and I had done it.

I came off the roof as fast as I could to check him over. There was a little blood, but it wasn't bad. With genuine concern I got my first-aid kit out, put some antiseptic ointment on the cut, and bandaged it up. It would heal and everybody knew it; these people have seen a good deal more than this.

But the incident wasn't closed. Everyone was waiting. Tense. Troubled. Expectant.

People continued what seemed like bickering back and forth, all in high-volumed excitement. I couldn't understand enough language to make sense of it, and I didn't know what else to do.

Wei Ali was still agitated, standing there with his new bandage and his torn shirt. I looked at that shirt. It had never been any great piece of fabric, and it looked like it had seen long service of almost daily wear. But now it wasn't simply old, it was *torn*.

Maybe if I paid for it, I thought, *that might make him feel better*. With all eyes following my every move, I went over to my bags, fished out a couple of *kinas* 'dollars' and gave them to him.

As soon as I did that, in full sight of everyone as it was, everything changed. He smiled broadly and everybody quieted down. Justice had apparently been covered. I had done the right thing. Everything was even again and we were all back to normal.

As far as I was concerned, I had only showed appropriate concern. The wound needed dressing; I dressed it. The shirt needed replacing; I gave him some money. But to them it went far deeper than that.

Accidents don't just happen around here, or at least they aren't passed off as easily as that. For every act of harm, whether intentional or accidental, there always has to be some sort of compensation to even out the score.

All this was my first encounter with payback, the most basic of underlying structures in traditional Melanesian societies. In the past it was always the basis for tribal warfare—the continuous cycle of vendetta killings. These have always been "eye for eye, tooth for tooth" societies. When I inflicted injury, I had not only done damage, but caused a loss of face as well, and I had to pay. The money wasn't so much to replace the shirt as to make things right. It was a matter of moral restitution.

With such a system in place, it's easy for people to see how restitution is necessary when God has been offended. One man may sin against another, but ultimately the sin is against God. He is the One who has said do not lie, do not steal, do not commit adultery. When we break those laws something has to be done, not just in compensation to the person offended but to God Himself.

The fact that we're powerless to do this and that God took the initiative and sent His Son to do it for us, is what the gospel is all about. The Folopa know this, at least those who have listened to the Talk do. The death of Jesus is the payback for our offenses. He paid the price that was too heavy for anyone else. That Jesus suffered and died—willingly and terribly—is very meaningful to the Folopa. Somehow they are more tender toward that truth than we are. It doesn't take much to send them into a deep silence of contemplation.

It was years after that first encounter with payback when we translated Luke 22. It wasn't an easy passage to handle. Jesus was with His disciples, observing the tradition of Passover for the last time. All the symbolism of the slain Passover lamb would shortly be fulfilled in His own death. He would become the appeasement before God for the sins of men.

With the completion of these old symbols, however, He introduced new ones to serve as reminders. The bread would stand for the breaking of His body and the wine for His spilled blood.

> And he took bread, gave thanks and broke it, and gave it to them, saying, "This is my body given for you; do this in remembrance of me." In the same way, after the supper he took the cup, saying, "This cup is the new covenant in my blood, which is poured out for you" (Luke 22:19-20).

We had some difficulty with the word for body. Because of customary usage that had preceded us, they wanted to translate it *mi* 'meat'. That's how the pastor who came here talked about it, they said.

Communion services among the Folopa are very solemn. Without any grapes or bread in the area they use sweet potato and lemon juice instead. It's all they have, and it is enough.

In translating, they explained to me how the lemon

juice stands for blood and the sweet potato stands for meat. It made sense to them since they saw meat and blood as parallel terms.

I saw their point but had to disagree. That was *not* what the Bible was saying. The Bible is talking about body, not meat, and the word for body is *tiki*.

We discussed this for some time. I saw how easy it would be to employ the term "meat" and think it was perfectly right. Especially here. Papua New Guineans have had a history of eating meat—and human meat at that. It would be a natural tie in . . . but that was not the meaning Jesus intended when He said, "This is my body."

It was in His body that He ministered on earth, that He took the abuse, that He died. It was an act of His whole personality—mind, will, feelings, and spirit. His whole being suffered the penalty for our sins.

He took our punishment. On Himself. In His *body*.

As for "blood," that was pretty straightforward. Blood is blood. In the Bible blood is a symbol for life. It also has everything to do with the most solemn of covenants.

We translated "covenant" with the term for "binding agreement." But it was not easy to show how the blood was what made the binding agreement stick.

Jesus' saying, "This cup is the new covenant in my blood," was difficult to translate because the idea of blood having anything to do with a binding agreement was puzzling. How could an agreement be "in my blood"? Making it harder, the Folopa do not have any direct translation for "in." I looked at another version of the Bible in English and found the wording, "This is the blood of the covenant." That didn't help either!

Our Lord's original hearers had no problem with this—at least not with the language. "The blood of the covenant" was something clear in their culture and history.

But how to say it in Folopa?

It took us some time to get it. The fact that the Folopa had been observing communion for years without fully understanding it didn't help us. Finally we settled on using the word, *eratapó* 'to bring into being'. It would serve as the missing connector between blood and covenant. It was the blood that brought the covenant into being. It ratified the agreement. It made it happen.

The Folopa think about these things a great deal: that Jesus really lived, suffered, and died for them. And they think about it most when they observe communion—even though what it was all about had never been a complete connection. But now it was made clear—the blood was not just symbolizing a life put to death but was symbolic of God's agreement.

Agreements are usually between two people—here it would be between man and God. But as man is fallible and could not keep his side of it, God had to make the covenant with Himself, through His own Son.

Now, bound in the blood of God's Son, the agreement is permanent. The significance began to come through to the Folopa. In communion, we're not just remembering the actual, physical death of Jesus on the cross but observing again the agreement that God made with His Son for our sakes.

The payback has been paid in full. It is a revolutionary truth in any society—but particularly so where payback is everything.

It's *beté* at the deepest level.

19

Ransom

(Mark 10:45)

Jesus died, but not for nothing.

He died as a ransom for many. He told about it on several occasions before it happened. He wove it into his teachings on how his followers are to live, which is almost always the opposite of what our natural sense would tell us. Such came out in the passage we were working on in Mark:

> "Whoever wants to become great among you must be your servant, and whoever wants to be first must be slave of all. For even the Son of Man did not come to be served, but to serve, and to give his life as a ransom for many" (Mark 10:43-45).

Ransom, ransom, I thought, *what is the word for ransom?*

This is the heart of the gospel—the *beté* of the whole message.

The men around the table had that common blank expression on their faces that must have reflected my own. *Here we go again,* they seemed to be thinking. *He's looking for a word. What is it?*

It was often like this. A game of twenty questions.

"I'm thinking of something and you've got to tell me what it is."

"Do we get any hints?"

"I'll try," I said. "Back to the fighting days. You took captives, right?"

"Yes."

"Were there ever times when you offered to release the person alive—say, to trade the man or woman or child for whatever you could get, like shells or pigs or anything like that?"

The question was absurd to them. Their laughter sent hints of ridicule and I hesitated to probe again. To have ever considered something so materialistic was beneath them. Their wars and killings had always been to avenge death. It was just to keep the score even—period.

Hapele, however, was thinking and seemed to grasp what I was getting at. "We do have something like that," he said. "It's not quite the same. It was never used with an enemy, but we do use it between clans. It's *duputapó.*

I knew the word. It means "trade."

"Tell me about it," I said.

"You know," he said. "Things have to always be kept

even. But sometimes you can't keep them even, not perfectly, when your own people are involved. It's like what happened with Wótale," he said.

"What happened with Wótale?" I asked.

"Well," he continued, "not long ago we were making a new garden and Wótale was cutting one of the big trees. Just down the hill from him a woman was working sago. They knew of each other's presence and Wótale kept warning her to move, but she wanted to get a little more done first. She knew it was going to take a while to get that big tree down, so she kept working.

"When Wótale finished the undercut he yelled to her again but she still didn't leave. Then suddenly—and earlier than either of them expected—the tree groaned and began its fall. He yelled and she ran, but there was no way to get clear. The tree fell right on her, crushed her skull and she died.

"What followed was a terrible uproar. Wótale got out of there as fast as he could, hiding himself in his men's house and all the clansmen of the dead woman immediately went for their bows and arrows and axes. As one body they marched up to Wótale's longhouse and stood outside yelling and shouting and demanding justice. They were calling for Wótale's life for the life of the woman he'd killed.

" 'But it was an accident,' his clan brothers protested from inside the longhouse.

" 'It doesn't matter. He did it,' they all shouted back.

" 'But he warned her!' they yelled out.

" 'That's no matter!' they yelled back.

"Wótale never came out, but after awhile his clan brothers did, and they brought things with them. They began spreading objects out on the ground, starting with pieces of bark cloth, *kina* 'abalone' shells, red cloth, axes, bush knives, salt. They were all valuables, things they would never give up except under great duress. They also drove stakes in the ground and tethered pigs to them.

"As the stock of goods kept growing, the woman's clan didn't subside in their yelling threats, and Wótale's people were doing a lot of yelling back. It was all bargaining and bickering for how much it would take to pay for a life. It went on and on at high pitch until somebody from the woman's clan yelled, '*Supó*.' "

Supó means "enough!"

"Then the leader of the men's house said, '*Duputapó*.'

"That completed it. There was a trade. The bereaved clan picked up all the valuables, leading the pigs on their tethers, and went home. Then Wótale came out into the open and was free to resume normal life without fear of further reprisal."

"How would it be if we used that word in this verse?" I said. I wrote out something rough: "We were in jeopardy of being killed but Jesus came to make a trade. He gave His life up instead and we got to go free."

"*Duputapó*." Hapele nodded. "And God said, '*Supó*.' "

"That's right."

One of the old men had been listening intently. He leaned forward, a big *kina* shell swinging on his bare chest.

"That's hard to believe," he said.

"What is?" I said.

"That *duputapó* was a person. In the past we've given a great deal to trade for a clan brother. A great deal. But we've never given a person. And a person would never give himself!"

He looked around at the others, the whites of his eyes flaring in deep-set sockets. He leaned back with a sigh, like it was beyond his grasp. Then he said what they always say when things hit them at the deepest level: "We are dying of the deliciousness of this talk."

20

Hate Your Brother

(Luke 14:25-26)

Τhat's good," they said. "That's really good. . . ."

They always liked to encourage me after a translation session. But this time I sensed a "but" coming.

We'd been working on Luke. Jesus was at the height of His popularity. Large crowds followed Him with enthusiasm, though some were not genuine or were not thinking about any cost. At one point He turned and said:

If anyone comes to me and does not hate his father and mother, his wife and children, his brothers and sisters—yes, even his own life—he cannot be my disciple (Luke 14:26).

We'd translated that into good Folopa and the men

were giving their approval. "That's good," they said, "but there's one little thing you've got to change. It's just a small thing. Just a word. Everything else is good. You don't need to change anything else, but there's one part you've *got* to change."

"All right," I said, "what part is that?"

They smiled a little. "Well, the meaning is mixed up. The way you translated it there, it says, '*Unless* a person hates his father, mother, wife, children, and all, he cannot be My disciple.' "

"Yes," I said.

"But what you *should* have said is, '*If* a person hates . . . he cannot be My disciple.' "

I suppose I should have seen it coming but I hadn't. I could see what they meant. They knew enough about the gospel at this point to know that love is the key, not hate.

The basic value of love, or at least that of supreme loyalty is not new to them. Clan ties and family ties are stronger than Super Glue in these parts. And so they have always been.

The brother–brother relationship is very tight in all Folopa culture. The same carries over into other relationships where certain cousins are bound together as if they were brothers. Each of these special relationships involves strict expectations and obligations. One does not get angry with his brother, for example. Rather he promotes harmony and always seeks peace. He always shares food and possessions with his brothers; he is available to help whenever he's needed in hunting or gardening or house building; he makes the marriage proposal for his brother's chosen bride, and he leads the hunting trips to get game for the bride price. In a fight, he holds his brother back from doing bodily harm to another.

When a man dies his brother will show the greatest empathy with deep grief and anger. He won't rest until he has personally learned the cause of death (like who did the sorcery) and has seen that revenge is taken. He will mourn his clan brother's death for at least a year.

For each of the family relationships, there are expectations, established since before anybody can ever remember. Each has its role, and breaking it means violating the unwritten code. All this was the background into which Jesus was making His statement about counting the cost.

"Yes, you're right," I said. "Of course you can't be a disciple if you're going to hate someone. I know it and you know it. But the trouble is, this is what the Lord really said: 'Unless you hate your father and mother, wife and children, brothers and sisters, you cannot be My disciple.' We did *not* translate it wrong."

They looked at me, I looked at them, and none of us knew quite what to do next.

They were convinced I had made an error. "Correcting" it would have been easy, involving only a small change in the Folopa from *hónitepa* 'if you do not hate' to make it *hótepa* 'if you hate.'

They were sure I was wrong—and I knew they would not be ready to go on until I fixed it. It opened a metaphysical dialogue that lasted for two days—the kind of conversation that can be stimulating (or frustrating) in any company.

Though it was a long struggle I finally managed to convince them that language problems were not the issue in this case. Jesus really had said it as we'd translated it—but

He didn't mean what they thought He meant when He said it.

"But then, exactly what *did* He mean?" they asked.

"Well, it doesn't mean that we're supposed to hate people," I told them, "and it certainly doesn't mean that if we hate people enough, then we can be disciples."

"But that's what you are saying it says!" they answered.

It was difficult. Looking for a way to explain it, I referred to all the commentaries and translator's handbooks I had at hand. As always, I worked at the exegesis, trying to get at the meaning of the original statement in the original context.

Any sort of diluting it down wouldn't work. Saying things like, "You've got to love these relatives and clansmen *just a little bit*, or, *not quite as much* as God," wouldn't do. It kept coming out like, "If you can just dislike people a little bit then you can be my disciple." Nothing was making sense.

During those days the village was embroiled in a court case with the people of Woposale. A man from the Fukutao area had died. He'd been having health problems and when he became very ill, men from the village had taken him down to the clinic at Woposale. But since he was beyond any help they could give him in the clinic, the medical workers arranged a flight to Mendi. That fifteen-minute trip by air saved twenty days by foot, which the man could never have survived. The expenses were picked up by the government, as is done in such cases. So was the operation. The doctor at Mendi performed a colostomy. But it all happened too late. The man died in the hospital.

As per the people's custom, the man's body was returned to his home—first via plane, then by stretcher pole for the day's steep walk up from the airstrip at Woposale.

"At least," said one of those who'd been with him in the hospital, "he died peacefully."

But this wasn't enough for his sons. They couldn't leave it at that; they had responsibilities to perform. They had to know who'd killed him. Conveniently the shaman lived right in the same longhouse. They went to him to get to the *beté* of the matter.

As a shaman won't stay in business if he doesn't know the answers to these things, he did his divining and found out who was responsible. The answer: It was a person in Woposale who had done it, and it was done by poison.

Whether it was actual poison or some nonphysical occultic substance, didn't matter much. What mattered was that a guilty party was identified and vengeance must be performed.

Courts in rural areas of Papua New Guinea are composed of village leaders called councilmen, selected by the villagers and approved by the national government. One respected man from each of several villages comprise the court, the presiding judge being that one with the least bias in the particular case.

These courts understand their own culture and when a case comes before them that involves murder by poison or sorcery it's not taken lightly.

Circumstantial evidence is brought forth. Possible motives are evaluated. In this case a statement was sought from the doctor in Mendi. When they asked him, he said he'd done what he could. He had performed an operation.

The sick man's health had improved for awhile but the problem was worse than that. He said he had given medicine but the disease proved stronger than the medicine.

That wasn't good enough for the court, at least not for the accusers. One of these wanted the doctor to sign a statement stating that the death was caused by poison. The doctor would not do that and the case continued to gather heat. Back in Fukutao some of the men were getting their weapons out, even their spears—a sign of real business.

It was during this time that we were debating that one verse. "It's not that Jesus wants us to not love anyone," I was still explaining. "He wants us to love everyone."

Yes, they all agreed with that.

"Basically what He was saying was that when it comes down to a contest of allegiance, God must win. When things come to an issue of who is going to have the final word in my life—my closest kinsman or God—it always has to be God."

They nodded.

"Jesus said it the way He did, with those particular words because there will be times when because of what you're doing, it will *appear* in the eyes of your family and clansmen that you hate them. That will happen because you'll be doing what God wants and not what they want."

Finally Whęare spoke with the clarity we'd been searching for. "Jesus," he said, "was not saying we're supposed to hate our family or our clansmen or anyone else. In following Him there will be times when we act in such a way that they think that because we follow God's will instead of theirs, we must hate them."

He said that with the clearest Folopa that could be uttered. The men looked around at each other and it seemed like finally, the clouds were breaking up. But they were heavy clouds indeed. These were issues in the very cords of the society. Could a society last with such truths? Brothers were to stand for brothers, right or wrong. Yet, was *that* always right? The system as it stood was always full of turmoil, that was sure, but to go against it was to go against everything. Wasn't there an easier way to be a disciple?

"It's another *beté*," Whęare said. "It's the *beté* of being a disciple. And it goes against what we've always held as the *beté.*"

———❦———

Talk of the battle continued to build outside. The men in the Bible house, though most of them were Christians, were expected to take part like everyone else—that's what clans are for.

That day when all the men walked out, Whęare stayed a few more minutes. I could see he was deep in thought.

Finally he said, "Do I go?"

"Do you go where?"

"With the men," he said. "To Woposale."

"Do you believe the word of the shaman?" I asked.

"No."

"Did the man die of sorcery?"

"I don't know . . ." Then he added, "No. The shaman works for the devil. He hates the Talk. He works against it. If I go I'll only justify him."

"Well?"

"But the man who died was my clan brother. If I don't go, what will they think? That I didn't love him? That I don't care about his death? They might even conclude that if I don't get involved, I must have had a part in it."

He picked up the sheaf of papers we'd just been working on and read. "Unless a person hates his brother . . ." His mouth thinned. His eyes glazed a bit.

"I have to go," he said. "Maybe I'll just not take my weapons. But then they'll think I'm a weakling. What can I do?"

I just looked at him. This battle had to be his.

In the end he went. I heard later that there had been a big show of force with lots of emotion. They were after justice and they would show their anger until they got it. But nothing happened. When they came back the next day I asked Whęare how it went.

"Bad," he said. "The court went bad."

"How?"

"Nothing happened. It broke up. A council from another village came in and said there wasn't enough evidence. He told everybody to go home."

"So that's the end of it?"

"Yes." He paused. He didn't look very happy.

"What is it?" I asked.

"The whole thing was wrong in the first place," he said. "We should never take that shaman's advice. It's from the wrong source. He keeps us running in circles, never settled, always angry.

"I went down there," he said, "but I didn't take my

weapons. I thought maybe I could be a peacemaker. But I wasn't. Nobody was. The whole thing failed. On the way back everybody was miserable. And they liked me least of all."

"Why?"

"You know. Because I wasn't really with them."

"I suppose they'll get over it," I said.

"I suppose. But that's not the worst."

"No? What's the worst?"

"It's like what the Lord said. You can't do both. You can't compromise. It's got to be one or the other."

21

Watersheds

(Acts 2-5)

Back in 1973, when we first came, there was a great influx into the church in Fukutao. The little building was jammed, there was lots of singing, and everybody was excited. But then a young man named Feléri died very mysteriously. He had a wife and a small child and had been one of the most dedicated Christians around. The death was a blow to everyone. What did it all mean?

People had been listening to what the pastor from Yonape was teaching: If you're a believer you may die, but that's nothing to worry about because you go to heaven.

Some people doubted the reality of that. Feléri would be a perfect test case, they reasoned. If anybody was a Christian, this young man had been. So, after he was dead awhile they went to his grave and dug his body up. When they found the corpse still there, they said, "It's all a lie."

This event, the dying of a dedicated believer and the subsequent discovery of his body by those who weren't versed in the meaning of their faith, marked a time of attrition in the church. There was a significant dropping away. Of course, the kind of Christianity many of the people had idealized simply wasn't real. It promised everything and demanded nothing.

The pastor stepped in and said, "There's some misunderstanding here. It's incomplete. I said the Christian goes to heaven, and this man has. That body you found in the grave is like the skin of a snake when it molts. The body is there but the real man has gone to heaven."

But they didn't want to buy that. That wasn't part of their philosophy. With them the body and the spirit were intertwined, especially in the bones. That's why they always used to carry human bones around. And when they found this young man's bones still in the grave they figured he must still be there.

That's what was happening when we first came. I suppose it was good. At least it clarified things a bit—on both sides. Even the Christians came a little closer to reality and saw that it wasn't all going to be easy after all.

Understanding had deepened since those early days. There was now more maturity than to dig up a body to see if it had gone to heaven. At the same time, the concepts were still complex, with potential for real unsettling if taken at the face value they demand.

From Genesis to Acts we had seen a steady increase of interest in the translation process. Starting with two at the table besides myself, we'd gone to twelve, then sixteen. I'd tried to hold it there but so many wanted to be a part of this unraveling of *beté* that finally I opened the doors to forty men—and then for Acts, to forty-eight.

They loved it. Every day they'd come to follow the events, gathering excitement from the growing drama and strength from the apostles—as those apostles gathered strength from the Holy Spirit. The momentum had been growing for days, starting with the power that came at Pentecost—with Peter standing and preaching to the crowds in spite of the presence of the Jewish leaders who wanted to snuff the whole movement out. Three thousand people believed on one day. The apostles performed miraculous signs and wonders and everybody was filled with awe.

The men loved this. In the Bible house the apostles grew in stature by the day and by the hour. When the men saw that Peter and John were unschooled and ordinary men, yet displayed such courage in the face of the religious powerbrokers, they loved it all the more.

There was an obvious competition going on. On the one side there were the scribes and Pharisees and on the other were the apostles. The stakes were high but there was no question as to who was winning. The apostles, what with miracles and angelic help at unexpected moments, could not be beaten.

We kept translating, discussing every passage, not going so fast as to not get it right but pushing ahead with eagerness for the sake of the drama. If, for some reason, one could not come for a day or two, he'd ask one of the others to keep him abreast of developments in the story.

One day as the apostles were released from prison they

went back to their own people to pray. When they finished praying, the very place where they were meeting shook on its foundation. To the men in the Bible house it was another sign that these Christians were invincible. Their power was straight from God. They could not lose!

When Ananias and Sapphira plotted a deception, Peter saw through it and immediately they fell dead. Such was their authority in spiritual realms. Great fear filled the early church then. The merely curious began to keep their distance, though the people's respect for the Christians continued to grow. People brought their sick and laid them on mats in the street so that at least Peter's shadow might fall on some of them as he passed by. As we continued translating, Peter grew to gigantic proportions in the minds of the Folopa.

There was a momentary low point when the apostles were thrown in jail. The Folopa know something about jail and it's not very good. It's dark, locked, without fire or warmth, and with little food—a removal from all the things the Folopa need and love. But then when the apostles were supernaturally sprung, leaving egg on the face of the religious leaders, everybody in the Bible house was laughing and saying things like, "These men have real power." "They have *beté!*" "You don't want to mess with these apostles!"

The captain of the guard and his officers accosted the apostles as they were preaching openly and brought them before the Sanhedrin. "We gave you strict orders not to teach in this name," they said, "yet you have filled Jerusalem with your teaching and are determined to make us guilty of this man's blood." When Peter and the others defended themselves, testifying again to Jesus and His resurrection from the dead, the elders were so furious they wanted to put them to death. But Gamaliel, a Pharisee and an honored teacher, warned against it, advising to let them go. "If their purpose or activity is of human origin, it will fail," he said, "but if it is from God, you will not be able to stop these men; you will only find yourselves fighting against God."

For the men in the Bible house, this was the ultimate statement. You fight against the apostles, you fight against God! Where's the contest? There can be no doubt on the outcome. It looked like finally the Jewish leaders were catching on. People get healed; people drop down dead; when the apostles pray the house shakes; when they're thrown in jail they get sprung free. They're not afraid of anything. They're giants. They're invincible. Next to them the opposition looks like grasshoppers. Essentially, Gamaliel's wisdom had been: If the *beté* of the matter is from men it will fall apart by itself, but if the *beté* is from God, look out!

"His speech persuaded them," we translated, and everybody yelled the Folopa version of, "All right!"

The next verse: "They called the apostles in and had them flogged."

Suddenly all the cheering and excitement gave way to silence.

"Flogged?"

"Yeah."

"That can't be right," they said. "Are you sure you have the right word?"

"Yes," I said. "*Fokosó salepó* 'flog', past tense."

They verified it was the right word, but couldn't believe

it was the right concept. They were stunned. Going to jail was one thing, but *flogged?*

———— ❦ ————

It was late in the day but the darkness that suddenly gathered in the room was not because of the hour. Somehow the score had changed in a most drastic way. Up until now the apostles had amassed hundreds of points while the Pharisees and Sadducees and priests had zero. They had been enjoying cheering for their unbeatable friends. But now this.

The men sat stunned. Silent. Some were getting up to leave. Others had already left in their minds.

"Wait," I said, "there's one more verse here."

I hoped the rest of it would explain it all. I did a rough verbal translation of Acts 5:41: "The apostles left the Sanhedrin, rejoicing because they had been counted worthy of suffering disgrace for the Name."

In my mind that cleared it up, but to them I had now completely befuddled it and it was now making even less sense. I kept working at it, taking new approaches with the language to be sure I was communicating clearly. But it wasn't working. First of all they could hardly believe that their heroes had been flogged—that God, whom these apostles served, would ever allow that to happen. But then to be told that they *rejoiced* in the honor of it all was just too much to take in.

Flogging is not an honor; it's a shame. Those two ideas would no more go together than two north ends of a magnet. They repel. If you're counted worthy of something you get a promotion; you are honored or rewarded. But what honor is there in disgrace? Suffering disgrace is what unworthy people deserve when they've done something wrong.

I worked and worked trying to express what the Scripture was saying. I needed them to actually think the thoughts so they could give me the proper way to say it in precise Folopa. My literal word-for-word attempt was not convincing them. They thought there must be an error somewhere. To explain it I had to talk all around it.

"Actually," I said, "God knows what sort of mettle a person's made of, right?"

There were nods.

"And He knows His purposes." More nods. "And God has purposes for a person suffering disgrace because it's an identification with Jesus Christ who suffered disgrace." They knew that Jesus suffered disgrace and they didn't like that either, but somehow that was different.

"So," I went on, "when we as followers of Jesus are given the same treatment that He was given, in that case it's an honor."

The blank stares were coming back at me again. "God sometimes works it out that we may be counted worthy to suffer disgrace for the name of Jesus."

More blank stares.

"And in those cases, if we do not suffer the disgrace, that may mean that we are not worthy."

———◄━✖━►———

Not much light had returned to their eyes as we quit for the afternoon. We prayed and they all left.

In the end that became one of the hardest concepts we ever tackled at the translation desk. I could see their question. It is a paradox. Like getting a report card and the teacher says, "You've done very well so I've decided to give you an F." Or like a boss who would say, "You're doing a great job; you're fired."

It was a bit discouraging, though I suppose it was good. This is what real Christianity is all about. It's not always a high. But the hard times serve us. They show us who we are. They bring us face to face with our stand.

In many ways it was like the first watershed, after we first came. Here we were again, shaking up the ranks. The first part of Acts had been so glorious, so victorious and heartening to everyone who came along. But then there was this bitter pill. The apostles were flogged. Apparently Christians don't always win. Often they don't. Not by appearances.

After that some of the men didn't come back. I was sorry to see it. They missed the next verse.

Day after day, in the temple courts and from house to house, they never stopped teaching and proclaiming the good news that Jesus is the Christ (Acts 5:42).

The apostles had suffered a blow but they counted it all joy. There was something deeper at the source.

22

One of Your Own Poets

(Acts 17:16-34)

It was to be one of those red-letter days. A day of utmost significance.

Days like that most often come unannounced. The date on the calendar, of course, isn't actually red. The Folopa don't even bother with calendars.

But on this day . . . *this* day . . . something was about to happen.

We were on Mars Hill. Actually we were about ten thousand miles away from Mars Hill, but we were working on the passage in Acts 17 which describes what happened when Paul was on Mars Hill. Sixteen of us were in the Bible house, zeroing in on Paul's words as Paul zeroed in on the Greeks.

We'd left off where Paul had been sent down south after things got too tense up in Berea. The Jews from Thessalonica weren't content with just pressuring Paul out of their city, but had to come over to Berea to stir the crowds up against him there, too. As with most of Acts there was lots of drama. For the Folopa in the Bible house, it was hard to sit still waiting to learn what would happen next.

It was hard for Paul, too. While he waited in Athens for Timothy and Silas to join him, he would go down to the synagogue or the marketplace and talk to people. He was distressed with the profusion of idols he found in that city, a reputed center of sophistication and learning. After some days, certain philosophers started disputing with Paul and finally brought him out to the Areopagus. The Areopagus was the place where both Athenians and foreigners spent all their time debating the latest ideas.

Paul continued to boldly proclaim his message but set it in a context relevant to the situation. He built his case by beginning with how his listeners were thinking, reasoning with them on their own terms. That's a basic principle of Bible translation. Indeed, that's what it's all about.

It wasn't the easiest passage; the terms so familiar to the Greeks were not familiar to the Folopa. Meaning comes in different packages in different languages, and sometimes if a concept hasn't been one of significance to a culture, there's no package at all. The words simply don't exist.

At the Areopagus Paul started out with: "Men of Athens! I see that in every way you are very religious" (Acts 17:22).

We had a problem right there. In Folopa there is no word for the concept of "religion," at least not one neat little term like that. On the one hand, what with the heightened spiritual awareness that they grow up with, to them *all* life is religious activity; it's not something you only sometimes do. On the other hand, since spirits are to be favored and appeased for the evil they are prone to work otherwise, things that might be categorized as "religious" were not regarded as positive—and certainly not joyous.

After discussing the passage and the context for some time, we finally came up with something like, "I see that you are very much praying-all-the-time people." It was a start.

Paul goes on: "For as I walked around and observed your objects of worship . . ." (Acts 17:23a).

Bump! We were stuck again. Paul was diplomatic, calling the Greek idols "objects of worship," but what were *we* going to call them? We had no perfect term for worship. The Folopa language, however, does have some words that reveal a healthy regard for authority. The strongest of these is an expression which translates literally, "putting up as superior and dying under." It's a crucial term reserved for those in positions of authority, such as a patrol officer or the law of the land or a parent. It basically means to submit to; to acknowledge that the other one is superior and that this will not be challenged. What it does *not* imply, however, is any appreciation, love, or adoration. Indeed, before the coming of the gospel there was no hint in the culture that these two concepts could be unified in one package—one term. Still, we took this one, agreeing it was the best we could come up with for now.

As for "objects" of worship we used the expression "a pile of stone stood up." That was the closest thing they could think of for what the Greeks had used.

We continued: "I even found an altar with this inscription: TO AN UNKNOWN GOD" (Acts 17:23b).

We were bumping our heads against the rocks. In Folopa, there is no concept for "altar." Again, we had to use an expression of explanation, in this case "standing stones used for praying and burning animals upon."

Neither is there a word for "inscription," so we put down "a writing that had been carved in the rocks."

The action had slowed down as we were running into language obstacles left and right. Every phrase seemed to have some problem, or several. I looked up to see if I was losing my audience. Instead of being restless or distracted, however, the men seemed particularly anxious to stay with it.

So we forged ahead. So did Paul. He continued with an abbreviated history of the cosmos and the earth, and the things on which the Greeks liked to speculate.

Now what you worship as something unknown I am going to proclaim to you. The God who made the world and everything in it is the Lord of heaven and earth and does not live in temples built by hands. And he is not served by human hands, as if he needed anything, because he himself gives all men life and breath and everything else. From one man he made every nation of men, that they should inhabit the whole earth; and he determined the times set for them and the exact places where they should live (Acts 17:23c-26).

We worked our way through that. It was laborious but we were making progress. Obviously Paul was exercised. He knew that God wants to be worshiped in spirit and in truth and that those Greeks were falling fall short of this. He was convinced that people in Athens were not worshiping the right God. And even if they were tacitly acknowledging that such an "unknown God" might exist, they were not going about it in a way God would accept. He had provided the way through the death of His Son.

I sensed the men in the Bible house stirring with interest, though I wasn't sure why. There seemed to be some new anticipation, the kind of interest which usually caught fire in a passage of intense action. But this one had no action—not to speak of. I wondered about it. They'd known since Genesis that God started the human race and how it grew from one man to spread across the earth. But apparently something was hitting them afresh here.

I suggested we take a break, but they would have none of it. We kept moving.

God did this so that men would seek him and perhaps reach out for him and find him, though he is not far from each one of us (Acts 17:27).

I knew the term for "seek," but not for "reach out," or as some versions put it, "grope." To act it out I got up, closed my eyes and felt along the walls and table as if I was looking for something. They caught on. They're often in such a position in the men's house, when in the middle of the night—with no light and with the fires gone out—they have to get up for some reason.

I got the words, *sisité kutu beterapó.* It fit for what Paul was getting at: Without God we are lost and in the dark, but God has so ordered things that if we seek Him, He will be found. He is never far from us.

We moved on.

"For in him we live and move and have our being." As some of your own poets have said, "We are his offspring" (Acts 17:28).

The men nodded, some scratching their chins or putting their fingers to the center of the forehead in their classic gesture of pondering. But we were stuck again. We had no word for "poet."

Indeed, we were a long way from first-century Greece, where poets abounded—here we didn't even have a word for one. As I fumbled around trying to explain what a poet was, I fairly proved that I was not one myself—at least not in Folopa.

"A poet is someone who can talk well," I said. "His speech is effective and he makes the language sound good. The things he says are what people love to hear because he puts into words what they value and what they believe to be the basis of life."

"Oh," they said, "we have people like that. He's a man that's good at relating the old legends and stories. He knows things, and he knows how to say them. When people listen to him they say it is *delicious*."

There was still no word for it, but I wrote in the description: *Beté tuẹ muturaalu fo foso du betere whị.* It was interesting to find the word *beté* embedded in the long expression. A poet knows things that are basic and can express them.

The place got quiet again.

Every eye was either on me or on the words I was writing.

The sound of the pencil was all that broke the silence.

I looked around, still mystified at what *they* could be mystified about, took a breath, and plunged ahead.

Therefore since we are God's offspring, we should not think that the divine being is like gold or silver or stone—an image made by man's design and skill. In the past God overlooked such ignorance, but now he commands all people everywhere to repent. For he has set a day when he will judge the world with justice by the man he has appointed. He has given proof of this to all men by raising him from the dead (Acts 17:29-31).

We worked on that. The men were always ahead of me, giving me more information than I could handle in a moment, and it usually took me awhile to catch up. As I was getting it all straight, fine-tuning the grammar, they began talking among themselves. At the edge of my awareness I heard them talking about a *hupu képi* and a *wusiki,* two kinds of snakes that live in the area. As far as I knew none of that related to anything in particular that we were talking about, but then . . . everybody needs a little diversion now and then.

I blew eraser crumbs off my papers and we set into the last verses of the chapter.

When they heard about the resurrection of the dead, some of them sneered, but others said, "We want to hear you again on this subject." At that, Paul left the Council. A few men became followers of Paul and believed. Among them was Dionysius, a member of the Areopagus, also a woman named Damaris, and a number of others (Acts 17:32-34).

We finished. I put down my pencil. What we had was another succinct gospel message uniquely crafted for the ears of its first recipients. It was cross-cultural communication at its best. It made sense both for Paul, a God-oriented Jew, and the Greeks, known for their sophistication and philosophical probings. But would it prove a bit heavy to cross yet another cultural boundary? Would it make sense to the Folopa, two thousand years later in one of the remotest places on earth?

As I had been getting the last phrases down, glancing over my notes to make sure I'd be able to read my scrawl later, the buzz around me began to grow in volume. Several men stood up. They were all talking at the same time and with such excitement I couldn't make sense of it. Before I knew it, all sixteen of them were on their feet shouting like they'd just inherited fifty pigs!

I looked around and waited. There was too much commotion to make any sense out of it. Finally they turned to me and said, "Héto Ali, do you know what we're talking about?"

I had absolutely no idea.

"We're talking about what we just translated," they said.

They pointed at the papers scattered before me. "We're talking about the legend of the two snakes."

"*What?*" I asked, thoroughly baffled.

"The two snakes," they repeated.

I was really lost. It was my turn to be in the dark and their turn to enlighten me!

"There's nothing here about snakes," I said.

"Yes, there is," they said. "Don't you know the legend of the two snakes?"

"No."

"Would you like to hear it?"

Of course I would. So they all sat down and Apusi Ali became the spokesman.

"We young ones," he said, "like we here, we don't know, but the old ones who really know the old ways and the old stories . . . they say that back at the beginning of time, back when everything began, there were two snakes and they spoke.

"One of them was a *hupu képi* and he said one word: *Kepaayako, kepaayako,* meaning 'live on, live on.'

"The other was a *wusiki* and he said one word: *Sinako, sinako,* meaning 'die, die.'

"But when the *wusiki* said 'die,' the *hupu képi* slapped him across the face and said, 'Don't say that!' He knocked his jaw off sideways and to this day when we pick up one of those snakes and hold him upside-down his jaw goes off sideways. The old men tell that if the *wusiki* had not said 'die' we would not die."

Apusi Ali looked at me intently and said, "But we do die."

I nodded, still waiting for the connection.

"Death comes to the village often," he went on. "And when our loved ones, our children, our brothers, our sisters, our wives are taken from us, it's a time of great heaviness. When it happens the whole village feels it. Death is always so close to us. It's a terrible reality and a terrible reminder: We do die."

He stopped for a moment. In contrast to a few minutes before, the room was morbidly still, as if the crooked-jawed *wusiki* himself was slithering along the floor and there was nothing anyone could do to stop it.

"But . . . that's it," he said. "What we were translating just now—what Paul was preaching at the Areopagus, about the resurrection—*that's it!*"

As his voice rose, all sixteen of them joined in again.

Again they were all talking and looking at me, waiting for me to catch on. I didn't.

"What are you talking about?" I asked. "Why is this passage so exciting?"

It was a passage of remote history: philosophical, esoteric, couched in terms specifically for the Greeks of a long time ago. Of all the passages we'd translated, this would seem to have the *least* meaning for these people.

"It's all there!" they said. *"Right there."* They pointed at my English Bible and the notepad that now contained the same message in rough penciled Folopa.

"What's right there?" I asked. "What's in these words that makes you so excited?"

With that they settled back in and with great patience sixteen teachers tried to instill understanding into the mind of one student. They took me all the way through what we had translated that day, reading from my notes. When I had been writing, it had been to get the words, but they had been grasping a significance that was behind the words. They had been struck with an unfolding of something particularly unique to their own culture, though it had eluded me.

We started back with the "stones stood for praying . . ." the expression for "altar."

"We have these stones, too," they said. "They're under the floorboards of the men's house. You don't know about them, but they're there. People used to pray to them. Some people still do."

It was new to me.

"We also have a legend about how the whole world was divided up and the people distributed around the world."

Ah, I thought, *so that's why they got so quiet and attentive after we translated that section.*

"Then we worked on that part about poets and saw how in Paul's time they had people who made the language good, just like we have. God made use of the things those poets said to show that He had always been revealing Himself to them, even though they hadn't known it. And now we see that our ones who make the language good have been doing the same thing, even though we didn't know it and they didn't either."

Everybody sat there looking at me, wide-eyed, waiting for me to experience the same breakthrough. The fog was clearing bit by bit. I was beginning to see what was moving them so.

"God really does know us," someone said, and with that the room was full of joyful clamor again.

"But—what about the snakes?" I asked.

"Well," Apusi Ali started, "We've never been able to figure that out, either. The poets don't always make sense. The old ones talk about it. They say that if the *wusiki* had not said, 'die,' then we wouldn't die. But the *hupu képi* is the stronger snake and he said 'live.' He rebuked the *wusiki* and wounded him. So in the legend the good snake prevailed. But in life he didn't. We continue to die and in the end there is no hope for us. Something was mixed up—or hadn't been told yet.

"But when we came to that part where God gave proof to all men by raising one Man from the dead, it all came together. God knows us. He knows our legend. Now the legend makes sense, and best of all, because of what God has done through Jesus Christ, it is fulfilled!"

The excitement rose again and spilled out into the air until people started coming to the door from the path to see what was going on. Meanwhile I just sat there pondering. I had never heard of this legend; I didn't know it existed, and even now I felt it took no small poetic leap to make it work. But somehow to them it was clear as day. It was like God was doing the same thing here as He did through Paul on Mars Hill—reaching back into their past and making sense of symbols, the origin of which had been forgotten. But God knew.

It was like an arrow had been sent right through the Bible house window and landed in their midst. It was an arrow with a message on it; and that message was in their language.

From that moment—when that profound realization broke through—everything changed. They looked through new eyes at everything we had translated before. They saw more depth in everything we worked on afterwards.

They were exhilarated beyond words with the massive discovery *that God had been with them all along*—that He had left His footprints where they had never seen them before. They knew now more than ever that this Bible and its message was not some foreign import, some white man's religion, but that it was a personal message just for them.

From that moment on the Bible became "their book."

I gathered my papers to go but somebody said, "Let's sing." So we sang. With gusto. With reverence. Everybody was floating off the floor in the Bible house. When we finished the song they wanted to sing another and another.

Then they said, "Let's pray," and they did, all standing in a circle, all praying at the same time.

Finally the joyous gathering broke up and I went home to tell Carol and the family what had happened. As I walked it all began to hit me. I reflected back to the first days when I wondered if I could really do this. And then to see how God had used me—how He'd used all of us! I felt humbled to be a part of His plan for reaching the Falopa.

As it says in the passage we'd just been translating:

In the past God overlooked such ignorance, but now he commands all people everywhere to repent (Acts 17:30).

There's a sense of history there. There may have been an ignorance in the past, but now there's an opportunity for every person to repent and experience the resurrection of the dead.

It was on this concept, the resurrection, that many of the Greeks—the sophisticates of the world—faltered. Some sneered. Others said they'd listen more, later. And a few believed.

That was in Greece, on Mars Hill, a long way away, a long time ago, and a million cultural miles distant. But on this day, on a hill in the village of Fukutao, everybody present was believing. There wasn't a skeptic in the group. God had clearly spoken directly into Folopa history, Folopa culture, and Folopa thinking. His intimate knowledge and care for these man-forgotten people could not be missed. It could not be ignored. Everyone rejoiced.

And then I was home, through the open door, and shouting the news to my family.

We too, rejoiced.

Epilogue

At this writing (1991), the translation of the first draft of the New Testament is nearly finished. Before long the complete book will be checked, revised, checked again, and finally printed. We trust that God will use it well in the generations to come.

It has been a lengthy and difficult process, not just for Carol and me, but also for those Folopa people who have walked with us on the journey. We're highly grateful for the four who have committed themselves to continuing the translation work with us. They're doing this under the auspices of the Bible Translation Association of Papua New Guinea. Nationally run and organized, BTA oversees about twenty-five active translation programs, now including Folopa.

Ultimately these people will need the entire Bible, not just the New Testament. Many wish they had it now. In time they will be ready to do the translation work for themselves. Such has been part of our goal in working together with these men.

The real fruit of all this hard work, though, is what comes out in living flesh. That is the desire of God. That is the reason He went to so much expense for us. And as we see more clearly who He is, His glory and holiness, and understand what worship really is, the more we will live our lives for Him—whatever language we speak.

One day I was sitting on the porch of the men's house. Some of the old fight chiefs were there telling stories about the old days. A friend and colleague visiting from Ukarumpa was with me. He asked them a most penetrating question.

"Do you ever long to go back to those days and have things like they used to be?"

Their answer was at first stunned silence. Was this man serious? Finally they erupted. "*No!* We would never go back! They were terrible days. We lived with constant fear. We could never rest. We killed and we were killed. It was no life.

"Now we know God, the true *beté* of all things. Why should we ever go back to anything less?"

Appendix

Translating Three Key Terms: Worship, Holy, and Glory

By the time we had been at the translation process a dozen years, some of the men were ready to do significant chunks of it themselves. Whaao was one. Over time he'd picked up a good deal of English, and he'd been with me long enough to catch a number of key translation principles.

He certainly knew his own language. That seems like a given. Of course all the Folopa know the Folopa language. But just as in any gathering of people, certain ones excel in vocabulary or in the use of language. Whaao was unique in that way. He possessed a natural curiosity about words, which—though his questions would stump me at times—is a commendable trait for a translator.

Translation is always a deeper process than it would seem on the surface. It's rarely a word-for-word proposition. I'd always heard that anything that can be said in one language can be said in another because of the nature of language— that language is adequate to explain anything. But I've found this to be something of an overstatement.

A language develops around what people talk about. Words are labels for concepts, but if the concepts have never been considered, the words will simply not be there. Any new concepts introduced into the culture may require a great many words to express them, or creative comparisons with things already known. Sometimes, they still seem to be beyond describing at all.

Three times we ran up against such walls when Whaao was translating the book of John. They were highly significant concepts, too, central to the message of Scripture and what God says about Himself and our response to Him. The words in English are worship, holy, and glory.

Worship is a foreign concept in Folopa culture. They had an awareness of spirits—continually—but their attitude toward them was more of a manipulation. And, as we've seen, when they gave any thought at all to their meager god of creation, certainly it was not worship.

In truth, we hardly understand these words in English. Worship, at least when it's directed correctly, is all wrapped up with that which is holy and glorious—more words for which they had no concept. It was all part of the same problem.

Whaao and I had long discussions about it. Worship, I would tell him, is what happens when, by your actions and your attitude, you acknowledge the superiority of God. You give Him the respect, honor, and gratitude that are due Him. You recognize His holiness, His glory. That line of reasoning would take us right back into discussion of holiness and glory.

Holy means separate, distinct. God's holiness speaks of His transcendence, His set-apartness. When we are holy we are separated unto God, separate from sin, and have moral purity.

There was no word for worship in Folopa.

Glory is a complicated word and I had a difficult time explaining it. In the Scriptures, God's glory sometimes refers to brilliant light, as in Luke 2 when the angel of the Lord and the glory of the Lord shone around about the shepherds. But in other places it isn't talking about light at all but about the greatness of God, His super-human qualities and attributes. His glory rolls all these things into one.

When you come to see what this really means in a personal way, there is no response but worship. Anything else would be arrogance. In the Bible, worship often includes kneeling down or some bodily posture that acknowledges One greater than we are. The Magi did that at the birth of Jesus. The account says they came and worshiped. They bowed down and by their bodily posture acknowledged that this little Baby was superior to them, in spite of their greater age.

Whaao and I struggled over these things. I tried to find words for these concepts, and he tried to understand them. It was excruciatingly difficult, but I was much encouraged to see this Folopa man grappling with concepts which had never known expression in his language.

We prayed over it often.

Whaao was putting his best efforts into the translation, stretching his brain, praying in earnest, asking God for good ideas on how to translate these three specific words. We'd finally get beyond them, and then a week later he'd come back and say, "Neil, tell me again about glory. And what is worship? What is holy?" And we'd go at it again.

Finally we settled on some descriptive terms that would have to do for the moment though I am still not really satisfied that we have them. For holy, we use the concept of "separate (from sin), pure, and distinct." When we speak of God's holiness, we use the term along with several modifiers. In this way we seek to capture the transcendence and wonder that are God's alone. For glory we use the Folopa term *ere ala*, which emphasizes the uniqueness of a person. For worship we use an idiom that roughly back-translates "dying under God." It means lifting up His name and praising Him. "Dying under God" means to acknowledge by everything one does and thinks that God is superior.

These terms will do for now. There may be better ways. I'm hoping that God will give additional insight to these men as they continually refine our earlier work. It may come as they gain a deeper grasp of what these terms really mean. In the meantime, I see them struggling—in a healthy sense. Sometimes one will stand up in church and say, "There's a word in the Bible here, worship, and we're not doing it." Then they'll start describing what it really means to worship, who God is in His glory and holiness, and what He expects from us.

Once again, the Folopa are searching for the source, for the reality beneath. It is the deepest *beté* of all.

Notes

Chapter 1

1. In Folopa culture, after a person has become a parent, it is no longer proper to call them by their given name. Rather, they are known by the name of their firstborn child with the word *Ali* for "father" or *Hama* for "mother" following it. Since our first child's name was Heather, or in Folopa, Héto, I am known as Héto Ali, and Carol is known as Héto Hama. Young men and women without children continue to be called by their own given names.

Chapter 4

2. A Folopa marriage is an arrangement between two clans, more than just between two individuals. A man is required to marry outside of his clan. Marriage within the same clan is considered incest. When a young man likes a young woman, he sends one of his older brothers over to ask whether she is willing to marry him. If she wants to, then negotiations begin.

The woman's clan is the one giving up one of its members. As that is considered a loss, it has to be replaced with wealth. So the young man's clan gives an agreed on number of large pigs, shells, money, and other material things.

Though there is a standard price for a bride, various factors can raise or lower it. It goes up if the woman is from a powerful clan, or if she is very attractive or educated. The price goes down if she is not a virgin or if there is any slur against her character.

Extensive negotiations take place between the two clans. Above all, peace must be maintained and everyone must be satisfied that they have been adequately compensated. It is a very complex network, and they keep careful track, though without pencil and paper. Everyone that contributes to the success of the negotiations will need to be compensated at some future date. It's part of how clans are solidified and continue to work together.

It should be noted that as these marriages are not only the means of binding a man to a wife but also of binding two clans together. Divorce is rare—and very difficult. In such a case, the woman's clan would be required to give back everything they had received.

Chapter 11

3. In Fukutao, as in many places in Papua New Guinea, all men live together in a men's house. It's a long structure with a corridor down the middle. Down both sides there are sleeping mats alternating with fire pits. From the time they are half-grown boys, all males live in the long house. Up in the ceiling thatch they keep arrows, curing tobacco leaves, seed, yams, and torches ready to light when there's need. Women and children live in separate satellite houses around the men's house.

Chapter 12

4. In those days a battle-injured man had to sneak back secretly to his house. In his wounded state he was considered extremely vulnerable to ghosts. For however many months his healing

required he would stay shut up in his hut. Pregnant women were thought to be a particular danger to him—being seen by one could transfer her "heaviness" to him, all the worse now being already so burdened. When his body was finally healed he would wash himself, put on his body paint and battle decoration, and go out. Women would then look at him and say things like: "Was this the man who was wounded? It couldn't be. Look at him, he's as good as ever!"

Having a man restored again was a relief, but there was still sorrow for those who had not fared so well. Skulls and other special bones of the recently deceased hung in the houses, reminding families of the loss. When they would get grimy from the fire smoke they were taken down and wiped off with animal fat.

Sometimes a man carried the jawbone of one of his dead clan brothers around, hung at his side under his arm. As he'd go he'd speak to it, asking whether a particular person was guilty. If, when the carrier mentioned a name the bone oozed some last bit of liquid, it verified that this was the guilty one.

A widow might wear a *ye ona* around her neck. This is some body part of the deceased; a bundle of bones or the flesh of a hand. For the latter, the wrist joint was removed so that the hand flapped against its forearm as it hung over the necklace string. It would wave eerily with the rhythm of the mourner's steps.

Sometimes the skin of the deceased was smoked over a fire and worn by another as a cape. This was all part of attempting to gain strength from the person's ghost, as well as a reminder that this loved one was gone forever and the death needed avenging.

The sight of a mourning widow, covered with mud, her *ye ona* dangling from her neck, was enough to make a warrior's blood run hot. Revenge didn't necessarily mean killing the specific person responsible for a death. Anyone from the village would do. But to fail to avenge a death was to fail as a man. To repay a death with a death was the only right thing to do.